Sascha Longstreth, PhD, Sarah Garrity, EdD, and Lisa Linder, PhD

Developing and Implementing Effective Discipline Policies

A Practical Guide
for Early Childhood Consultants, Coaches, and Leaders

Gryphon House
www.gryphonhouse.com

Copyright

Bulk Purchase

Disclaimer

Table of Contents

Part One — About the Teaching and Guidance Policy Essentials Checklist: A Five-Step Process for Improving a Behavior-Guidance Policy

Part Two — Improving Your Behavior-Guidance Policy Using the TAGPEC

Appendices

Acknowledgments

We are indebted to Drs. Ann and Rud Turnbull for their thoughtful feedback regarding how the TAGPEC can better support the inclusion of children with disabilities and their families. We would also like to thank the teachers, directors, principals, coaches, and program leaders who have allowed us into their programs. We have learned a great deal from these partnerships, and we hope that this guidebook will provide practical advice and guidance to others who engage in this important work.

Introduction

How to best support children with challenging behaviors in early childhood classrooms is one of the most frequent training topics requested by teachers. Troubling data on suspension and expulsion in the early years has created an urgent need to develop systems that support the social-emotional development of young children. For almost twenty years, we have examined how high-quality behavior-guidance policies can be used to create an infrastructure that supports the social, emotional, and academic success of all children. This guidebook complements our book *Effective Discipline Policies: How to Create a System that Supports Young Children's Social-Emotional Competence* (Longstreth and Garrity, 2018), which provides clear, evidence-based information to early childhood program administrators about developing and implementing behavior-guidance policies that support teaching and learning and prevent and address challenging behaviors.

We intentionally use the term *behavior guidance* rather than *discipline* in our work with early childhood programs, and the distinction between discipline and behavior guidance is key to our philosophical approach. Rather than focusing on trying to *prevent* challenging behaviors, many discipline policies focus on what will happen *after* the challenging behavior has occurred. As a result, discipline is often synonymous with punishment. Unfortunately, using punishment and rewards to "guide" children's behavior is common in early childhood settings. Asking a child to move his card from yellow to purple, using time-out, and posting sticker charts are typical strategies used to control children's behavior.

Behavior guidance, on the other hand, seeks to prevent challenging behaviors and focuses on teaching children social-emotional skills such as self-regulation, cooperation, empathy, and responsibility. We believe it is the adult's responsibility to teach children how to get their needs met in ways that not only work for the child but are also socially acceptable. As we will describe in greater detail in chapter 3 of this guidebook, the TAGPEC and related five-step process for improving behavior-guidance policies is grounded in a humanistic approach (Maslow, 1943; Rogers, 1961) rather than in a behavioral approach to challenging behavior. Both prevention and teaching are central to our philosophy.

About the TAGPEC

At the heart of our work is the Teaching and Guidance Policy Essentials Checklist (TAGPEC), an easy-to-use checklist (see appendix A) that describes seven essential features of high-quality behavior-guidance policies for programs serving children from birth to eight years of age. We developed the

TAGPEC via an extensive review of the literature in the fields of general education, special education, early childhood education, early care and education, early childhood special education, educational administration, and school psychology. Since that time, we have continued to refine the tool via our ongoing research project in partnership with early childhood programs in a variety of settings.

The TAGPEC is used to rate the quality of a program's existing policy, and each essential feature of the TAGPEC includes specific criteria that should be included in a high-quality behavior-guidance policy. Using information gained through the TAGPEC and discussions with stakeholders, programs can then engage in the five-step process described in *Effective Discipline Policies* as they begin in this work. The five-step process provides concrete, step-by-step instructions for revising policies and creating systems that support children's social-emotional development.

This guidebook expands on that five-step process and shares what we have learned working with program directors, early childhood mental-health consultants, technical assistance networks, and quality-improvement coaches.

What's in This Book

This book is intended as a companion to *Effective Discipline Policies* (Longstreth and Garrity, 2018). It will guide you as you use the TAGPEC to assess and revise your behavior-guidance policy.

Part 1 of this guidebook provides an overview of the TAGPEC and of the related five-step process for improving your behavior-guidance policy. The first chapter describes why we focus on policies and systems, and why we believe the TAGPEC can help create an infrastructure that supports children, families, staff, and administrators. In chapter 2, we offer an overview of the TAGPEC and describe its seven essential features, along with examples of how we have used the essential features in our work. Chapter 3 reviews the five-step process and provides background information that will prepare you for the more in-depth description of this process found in Part 2. In Chapter 4, Lisa Linder, a clinical child psychologist with expertise in early childhood attachment and the role of early experiences, environments, and relationships on early childhood mental health, describes the consultative stance that is essential to forming collaborative and responsive relationships with teachers, families, and other program staff. This chapter also includes "Pause to Reflect" activities that we hope will support you as you think through the complexities of the consultative process.

Part 2 offers an in-depth description of the five-step process, beginning with chapter 5. Chapters 6 through 10 explain each of the steps in turn and describe how to use the worksheets found in the appendices. We draw from our own experiences to describe how we have dealt with difficult situations, and we provide examples of how to talk through complicated issues. In this section, we take a closer look at the process of implementing the TAGPEC's and its five-step process in early childhood education settings. The process of crafting and fully implementing a high-quality behavior-guidance policy often takes three to five years. In this sense, the steps that we present in this guidebook are more cyclical than linear. We expect a program will engage in the steps multiple times before a true shift in the program's discipline culture occurs. This guidebook is a resource for programs to use repeatedly as they move through the cyclical process.

Most important, however, this guidebook contains an updated version of the TAGPEC. We have also incorporated new guidance from the field, including an increased focus on equity and inclusion that reflects the National Association for the Education of Young Children's (NAEYC's) *Advancing Equity in Early Childhood Education* position statement (2019) and the recently revised *Developmentally Appropriate Practice in Early Childhood Programs Serving Children from Birth through Age 8* (NAEYC, 2022). We have been very fortunate to collaborate with our colleague and friend Lisa Linder, who is the executive director of the Healthy Early Years (HEY) clinic at San Diego State University. The HEY clinic is a counselor training facility focusing on young children and their families. Through this partnership, we have used the TAGPEC and its related five-step process as part of early childhood mental-health consultation. We have also worked with county- and state-wide organizations that have used the TAGPEC to examine the quality of behavior-guidance policies as part of their continuous quality-improvement efforts.

The appendices include the TAGPEC tool, worksheets to help you think through the steps and develop an action plan, and suggested resources.

We recommend that you use our books as a starting point for your work. In them, we offer an overview of our humanistic approach to behavior guidance, a chapter on the importance of culture and languages, the research behind the TAGPEC's seven essential features, and information about how to score the TAGPEC and use the five-step process to revise and implement high-quality behavior-guidance policies. In keeping with our humanistic approach to behavior guidance, we hope practitioners in the field of early childhood education use these books as they work to ensure systems are in place to support children, families, and staff to be their very best.

1

About the Teaching and Guidance Policy Essentials Checklist: A Five-Step Process for Improving Your Behavior-Guidance Policy

CHAPTER 1

A Focus on Policies and Systems

Josephina was thrilled to begin her new position as the director of a community-based preschool. After several weeks, however, she is feeling exhausted and unsure of whether she is the best person for the job. There have been issues with biting in the toddler classroom, and just yesterday a preschooler threw a chair during group time and injured another child. Several of the teachers frequently send children to her office for behaviors that Josephina considers developmentally appropriate, and others will call parents to pick up their children from school when faced with behavior challenges. Parent and staff handbooks give little guidance to teachers or families about the center philosophy or practices to follow when children exhibit challenging behaviors. The teachers tell her that they feel unsupported and stressed out. One parent is very angry because her son is the only child who is sent to her office for behaviors that she sees other children doing too, and other parents are upset because their children are getting hurt. Josephina has just been assigned a coach by her state's local quality improvement program, and she plans to bring up these concerns during their first meeting.

Why We Focus on Policies and Systems

We have focused our efforts at the policy or systems level of early childhood programming for several compelling reasons. Policies are an inherent component of effective and systemic service delivery and represent an intentional set of guiding principles designed to translate the goals of the system into practice (Longstreth and Garrity, 2018). We view policies as a blueprint that guides program leaders as they collaborate with key stakeholders to build an infrastructure that supports the goals and philosophy of the program. We also believe that high-quality behavior-guidance policies can help administrators ensure that all children learn the social and emotional skills needed to be successful, and that teachers, families, and administrators feel supported and valued.

To be considered high quality, behavior-guidance policies need to promote practices grounded in research on evidence-based practices that are inclusive and developmentally, culturally, and linguistically appropriate. High-quality behavior-guidance policies can also help address the troubling rates of suspension and expulsion in the early years. Policy initiatives and guidelines from the US Department of Health and Human Services and Department of Education (2014); US Department of Health and Human Services, Office of Head Start (2016); Child Care and Development Block Grant of 2014 (Pub. L. 113-186); and NAEYC et al. (2016) describe the importance of policy in preventing and addressing challenging behavior and decreasing rates of suspension and expulsion. More recently, the book *Developmentally Appropriate Practice in Early Childhood Programs Serving Children from Birth through Age 8* (NAEYC, 2022) has a strong focus on equity. The book shares how the field can best teach and support all children using strategies to eliminate the use of suspension and expulsion in early childhood programs. NAEYC's equity position statement (2019) explicitly describes steps program administrators can take to advance equity in their programs that include a focus on policy and procedures:

- Establish clear protocols for dealing with children's challenging behaviors, and provide teaching staff with consultation and support to address these behaviors effectively and equitably.

- Consider potential effects of implicit bias by regularly collecting and assessing data regarding whether certain policies and procedures, including curriculum and instructional practices, have differential impacts on different groups of children.

- Set a goal of immediately limiting—and ultimately eliminating—suspensions and expulsions by ensuring appropriate supports for teachers, children, and families.

These recommendations are very much in line with the essential features of the TAGPEC. Furthermore, the TAGPEC five-step process will help program leaders design and implement policies that promote equity and reduce suspension and expulsion in the early years.

Another reason to focus on the policy and the systems level is the need to shift from blaming individual children and families to looking at how systems do or do not support children and families. Terms such as *institutional racism*, *structural racism*, and *systemic racism* draw attention to historical, political, economic, and educational practices that uphold systems of oppression and preserve the status quo. Attention to these macro-level contexts is essential when considering children's behavior.

NAEYC's position statement *Advancing Equity in Early Childhood Education* (2019) proposes that equity requires understanding this broader societal context, these biases, and the ways in which historical and current inequities have shaped the profession, as they have shaped our nation. The biases we refer to are based on race, class, culture, gender, sexual orientation, ability and disability, language, national origin, indigenous heritage, religion, and other identities. They are rooted in our nation's social, political, economic, and educational structures. NAEYC's position statement on developmentally appropriate practice also addresses the importance of understanding development in context and the need for early childhood educators to "reflect on and address their own inherent biases and to help them provide developmentally, culturally, and linguistically responsive learning experiences to an increasingly diverse population of children" (NAEYC, 2020). When considering what this means, it is helpful to review the definition of *diversity* provided in the position statement:

> Variations among individuals, as well as within and across groups of individuals, in terms of their backgrounds and lived experiences. These experiences are related to social identities, including race, ethnicity, language, sexual orientation, gender identity and expression, social and economic status, religion, ability status, and country of origin. The terms *diverse* and *diversity* are sometimes used as euphemisms for non-White. NAEYC specifically rejects this usage, which implies Whiteness is the norm against which diversity is defined (NAEYC, 2020).

Revisiting this definition as we engage in our work has helped us to reflect on our own positionality as White women and to consider the ways in which our privilege may affect our interactions, interpretation of events, and relationships with program staff and families.

By focusing on systems and policies, early childhood program leaders can examine and address structural or systemic issues that prevent the provision of equitable experiences for all children and families and can develop policies that support the inclusion and success of all children. As noted by Kendi (2019), "a racist policy is any measure that produces or sustains racial inequity between racial groups" and "an antiracist policy is any measure that produces or sustains racial equity between racial groups." This distinction is critical given the data on preschool suspension and expulsion rates. Young boys of color and young children with disabilities are suspended and expelled for behavioral challenges three to four times as often as other children (US Department of Health and Human Services, Office of Civil Rights, 2014). Unfortunately, our research indicates that program policies fail to address the TAGPEC items related to culture and diversity, with an alarmingly few programs describing evidence-based strategies for supporting culture and language in the classroom, in their work with families, or in their quality-improvement efforts (Garrity and Longstreth, 2020).

NAEYC's equity position statement (2019) also describes the importance of building awareness and understanding of one's own culture, personal beliefs, values, and biases. We have also identified the need for self-reflection in our work with early childhood programs, and Part 2 of this guidebook contains tools and processes intended to support consultants and program staff as they engage in critical dialogue that can result in meaningful change. Chapter 4 of this guidebook specifically describes the importance of reflection and the need to step back and consider multiple perspectives. Our hope is that using the TAGPEC five-step process to examine behavior-guidance policies will support the examination of how program policies, practices, and curriculum can support children's social emotional competence and ensure equitable outcomes for all children.

DEFINING TERMS

In our work, we have noted a variety of terms used in the field to describe professionals who work with young children in educational settings. To provide clarity and consistency, we use the following terms throughout this book:

- **Educator:** any adult in a program who has been hired to interact with students, including teachers, paraprofessionals, cafeteria workers, and playground supervisors

- **Administrator:** an individual who is part of program leadership and is often (but not always) the program director or school principal

- **Consultant:** the individual who is leading the efforts to assess and revise behavior-guidance policies using the TAGPEC five-step process. This can be a consultant from outside the program, a quality-improvement coach, a center or program director, a principal, or any other leader in the field.

- **Positionality:** the ways in which differences in social position and power shape identities and access in society

- **Program:** any early educational organization whose purpose is to educate and care for young children from birth to age eight. Types of organizations that care for young children vary widely and may include schools, corporate child care, family child care, private preschools, community-based preschools, state-funded preschools, and faith-based preschools, among others.

- **Student-support professionals:** individuals who work with children, educators, parents, and administrators to provide multitiered interventions that support the development of all students. Student-support professionals may include nurses, psychologists, counselors, social workers, librarians, behavior specialists, developmental specialists (for example, occupational and speech therapists), and members of pupil-support services teams. Sometimes, the word *staff* will be used to refer to educators and student-support professionals collectively.

CHAPTER 2

The Teaching and Guidance Policy Essentials Checklist

> Josephina and her coach, Michelle, discussed Josephina's concerns and the frustration she was feeling in her new role as a center director. They identified the need for the program to have a clear philosophy that describes the program's goals, beliefs, and values about how children learn and develop. They also identified a need to build consensus about how to meaningfully engage families in the program and how to develop behavioral expectations that are clear and age appropriate. Josephina thought it was especially important for everyone to be on the same page regarding developmentally appropriate behavior and what to do when challenging behaviors occur. She also wanted to put strategies in place to prevent challenging behaviors, rather than just reacting to them after the fact. Michelle pointed out that working on these issues would require discussions among staff and family members about how beliefs, values, and assumptions often affect how individuals interpret and respond to children's behavior. Michelle introduced the TAGPEC and its five-step process as a way to address Josephina's concerns.

The Teaching and Guidance Policy Essentials Checklist (TAGPEC) and its five-step process (Longstreth and Garrity, 2018) is a tool for assessing program policies and supporting dialogue about a program's philosophy and practices on behavior guidance. The aim of the TAGPEC is to support program leaders, staff, families, and those tasked with supporting early childhood programs in developing policies that reflect what research tells us about how to prevent and address challenging behavior in the early years.

We have found the TAGPEC to be a useful tool in having conversations with program leaders about their program's strengths and areas of need. We have also found it helpful in supporting teams to engage in reflection not only about program goals, but also about their own cultural attitudes and behaviors that may affect how they view children's challenging behavior.

This chapter provides an overview of the TAGPEC, beginning with a description of our humanistic approach to behavior guidance and the five assumptions that guide our work. We then briefly describe the seven essential features of the TAGPEC and discuss how programs can use these essential features and items to create or revise behavior-guidance policies and engage in the process of continuous improvement. Additional information about the TAGPEC, including examples of high-quality policies and how the tool can be used to support a developmentally, culturally, and linguistically supportive classroom, is available in *Effective Guidance Policies* (Longstreth and Garrity, 2018).

A Humanistic Approach to Behavior Guidance

As noted in the introduction, we intentionally use the term *behavior guidance* rather than *discipline* when describing the TAGPEC five-step process; our approach to child guidance is grounded in a humanistic rather than a behavioral perspective.

Humanistic theories, introduced by psychologists such as Abraha`m Maslow (1943) and Carl Rogers (1961) in the mid-twentieth century, emphasize people's inherent ability to attain self-actualization— or their best self. The humanistic approach underlying the TAGPEC values each child's personal worth, agency, and creativity as they strive to reach their individual potential (Longstreth and Garrity, 2018). This approach is very much in line with the approach espoused by NAEYC's updated position statement on developmentally appropriate practice (2020) and their revised book *Developmentally Appropriate Practice in Early Childhood Programs* (2022). NAEYC's equity position statement, too, reflects our humanistic approach to behavior guidance as it recognizes that "All children have the right to equitable learning opportunities that help them achieve their full potential as engaged learners and valued members of society." Our humanistic approach also reflects the concept of dignity proposed by Turnbull, Turnbull, Wehmeyer, and Shogren (2020), who assert that all children, including those with disabilities, should experience dignity in their educational experiences.

The following list presents the five assumptions of our humanistic approach to behavior guidance.

- **The role of the adult is to teach children appropriate social-emotional skills.** Behavior guidance is preventive rather than reactive and focuses on teaching children effective strategies for expressing emotions and solving conflicts, and supports the development of self-regulation, empathy, and perspective taking.

- **Relationships guide and regulate behaviors.** Relationships are the foundation for teaching and learning in the early years, and positive relationships provide a powerful context for learning. Because problem behaviors occur within the context of the teacher-child relationship, they are best resolved within these relationships through the socialization practices of the teachers.

- **Behavior is communication.** A child's challenging behavior is a signal that something is not right. Children may lack the skills to express their needs appropriately, or they may be too dysregulated to use the skills they have. By identifying an unmet need or needs, adults can teach children to get their needs met in more socially acceptable ways.

- **Each child is a unique individual.** Multiple characteristics distinguish children from one another and make each unique. These characteristics are biological, familial, social, and cultural, and they intersect with broader economic, historical, racial, and economic contexts.

- **Implicit bias affects decision-making.** Implicit bias influences perceptions, interactions, behaviors, and feelings toward others in ways that we are unconscious of.

These assumptions are based on our belief that behavior guidance should be preventive rather than reactive and that children need to be taught social emotional skills in the context of responsive and caring relationships. Additional information about this approach, as well as examples of how it is implemented in practice, can be found in chapter 3.

The Seven Essential Features of the TAGPEC

The seven essential features of the TAGPEC (see Table 1) represent the broad topic areas we have identified as necessary for inclusion in a high-quality guidance policy, and each essential feature includes items that define specific criteria within that essential feature.

Each item on the TAGPEC is rated along three dimensions:

- A rating of *no* and a score of 0 is given if the item is not addressed in the policy.

- A rating of *emerging* and a score of 1 is given if there is minimal evidence the item is addressed in the policy.

- A rating of *yes* and score of 2 is given if the item is clearly addressed in the policy.

The highest possible score a program can obtain on the TAGPEC is a 68, indicating that all seven essential features and the corresponding thirty-four items are sufficiently addressed in the policy. Chapter 5 of *Effective Discipline Policies* provides additional information about scoring the TAGPEC, including exemplar policy statements for each item; appendix A provides the full tool.

ESSENTIAL FEATURE 1: INTENTIONAL FOCUS ON TEACHING SOCIAL-EMOTIONAL SKILLS

Items in the first essential feature focus on an instructional, proactive approach to behavior guidance that supports the learning and practice of appropriate prosocial behavior. The items reflect the need for teachers to be intentional about supporting children's social-emotional development by using multiple strategies that are developmentally, culturally, and linguistically appropriate.

Our experience and research (Garrity, Longstreth, Potter, and Staub, 2015; Garrity, Longstreth, and Linder, 2016) indicate that programs generally score high on this essential feature. We have found that programs need the most assistance thinking about strategies that are developmentally, culturally, and linguistically appropriate. We have added a list of resources at the end of the chapter that we have found helpful.

Social, Emotional, and Academic Success for All Children

EF 1 — INTENTIONAL FOCUS ON TEACHING SOCIAL-EMOTIONAL SKILLS

EF 2 — DEVELOPMENTALLY AND CULTURALLY APPROPRIATE LEARNING ENVIRONMENT

EF 3 — SETTING BEHAVIORAL EXPECTATIONS

EF 4 — PREVENTING AND ADDRESSING CHALLENGING BEHAVIORS USING A TIERED MODEL OF INTERVENTION

EF 5 — WORKING WITH FAMILIES

EF 6 — STAFF TRAINING AND PROFESSIONAL DEVELOPMENT

EF 7 — USE OF DATA FOR CONTINUOUS IMPROVEMENT

ESSENTIAL FEATURE 2: INCLUSIVE, DEVELOPMENTALLY, CULTURALLY, AND LINGUISTICALLY APPROPRIATE LEARNING ENVIRONMENT

We have updated this essential feature with an additional focus on the inclusion of all children. Items 5 and 6 are new and draw attention to the need for program policies to state a commitment to including all children and to explicitly prohibit discrimination based on a child's characteristics, such as race, sex, gender, or presence of disability. This essential feature focuses on the importance of behavior-guidance policies that support an inclusive, developmentally, culturally, and linguistically appropriate learning environment that is predictable, engaging, and relationship based.

In one program that we worked with, discussions about this essential feature led program staff to think deeply about what a strengths-based view of culture really means. They considered how classroom environments and materials could more accurately reflect the cultural traditions and values of the families and community and decided to add family pictures to the dramatic play area and several menus written in Spanish from community restaurants. The program's revised guidance policy described the staff's commitment to embracing the diversity of their community and to using accurate language when discussing human differences.

ESSENTIAL FEATURE 3: SETTING BEHAVIORAL EXPECTATIONS

This essential feature addresses the importance of early childhood behavior-guidance policies that describe clear and consistent expectations for behavior that are culturally and linguistically appropriate. While program-wide behavioral expectations are quite common in elementary school settings, they are less common in community-based early childhood programs. We have updated items 16 and 17 of this essential feature by changing the word *rules* to *expectations*, based on feedback received from programs. This change also allows for consistency between program expectations and classroom expectations. We have found it helpful to provide examples of what behavioral expectations look like in action.

For example, for a program whose expectations were, "We are safe. We are kind. We are respectful," we included the following examples in the behavior-guidance policy:

- Jose's mother tied DeShawn's shoe. That was very kind.

- When we put the toys away, we are being safe.

- When Luna asked Ronald to use the glue, she was being respectful.

- Miss Sofia thanked Miss Tomeka for bringing her the book. That was kind and respectful.

ESSENTIAL FEATURE 4: PREVENTING AND ADDRESSING CHALLENGING BEHAVIORS USING A TIERED MODEL OF INTERVENTION

This essential feature draws from positive behavioral support (PBS) models and describes the need for early childhood behavior-guidance policies to identify primary, secondary, and tertiary preventive and intervention practices that are culturally and linguistically appropriate. In item 20, we have added response to trauma as a possible reason for children's challenging behavior and have more fully explicated possible tier 3 strategies—individualized, intensive interventions for a very small number of children with persistent challenges—by adding functional behavioral assessments and referral for additional assessment as possible strategies. Items 24 and 25 are new and describe the need for intra- and interagency collaboration and a policy statement related to privacy and confidentiality.

Our work with programs and our research (Garrity, Longstreth, Potter, and Staub, 2015; Garrity, Longstreth, and Linder, 2016) have shown that programs generally have tier one and tier three interventions described in program policy. However, guidance policies often skip from describing the importance of relationships and the need to teach children social-emotional skills to detailing the steps to take to remove a child from the program once challenging behaviors occur. To address the lack of tier two interventions, one program decided to insert a live link to resources provided by the Pyramid Model Consortium (https://www.pyramidmodel.org) in its description of second tier strategies. The strategies offered on the consortium website, such as scripted stories, the solution kit, and ways to engage families, all support teaching social problem-solving strategies with children who need a bit more support developing their social-emotional skills.

ESSENTIAL FEATURE 5: WORKING WITH FAMILIES

This essential feature discusses why early childhood behavior-guidance policies should reflect joint decision making, family priorities that foster family quality of life, and the needs of all family members. We have added the term *authentic* to item 26 to underscore the importance of learning with and from families. In our experience, programs do not score very high on essential feature 5, with items 28 and 29 being the most challenging. The program policies we have reviewed typically do not address embedding family's cultural practices and routines into behavior-support plans and fail to make connections between home and school. It is important to remember that the TAGPEC five-step process is designed to support ongoing reflection and continuous improvement, and programs often select TAGPEC items as goals they hope to attain in the future. One program-guidance policy described the intention to include families in the development of behavior plans in the following way:

> Families will be asked to share information about their beliefs and values about children's behavior and routines and practices that are culturally valued at home. Families are asked to incorporate the goals of the Intervention Plan into family/home routines whenever possible to ensure consistency between home and school.

ESSENTIAL FEATURE 6: STAFF TRAINING AND PROFESSIONAL DEVELOPMENT

Essential feature 6 describes the need for early childhood programs to commit to providing ongoing staff training and professional development on implementing the behavior-guidance policy. We have added the terms *equity* and *inclusion* to item 32 to reflect our increased focus on these issues. Programs frequently receive a score of zero on this item. Our work over the past few years has highlighted the critical need for reflection and the importance of providing space and time for program staff to identify and address their own biases. Chapter 3 of this guidebook provides many useful strategies for reflection and tools to help consultants create a reflective space that allows for hearing and integrating different perspectives.

ESSENTIAL FEATURE 7: USE OF DATA FOR CONTINUOUS IMPROVEMENT

Essential feature 7 discusses why it is important for programs to use a data-collection system to evaluate the relative success or failure of the behavior-guidance policy. We have found, in both our research and our practice, that programs typically receive a score of zero for this feature.

Item 34 now includes another critical reason for data collection: pinpointing concerns and tracking the program's progress toward meeting their goals about preventing and addressing children's challenging behavior. For example, one center we worked with was required to complete a self-assessment of the program every June as part of their contract with the state. The director and her team decided to review documents related to behavior (referrals, behavior-guidance plans, results of developmental screenings) every year as part of this annual assessment, thus ensuring that data would be used for continuous improvement and would be integrated with other quality-improvement efforts.

A Process, Not a Product

We are very aware of the underresourced and undervalued nature of early childhood education in the United States. We understand that there may be items on the TAGPEC that are out of reach for some programs. For example, a small, community-based preschool may not have the resources to conduct developmental screenings on all children. Or, developing and/or executing a memorandum of understanding with a local school district may come with a host of challenges. The aim of the TAGPEC five-step process is for programs to engage in dialogue and develop a policy that works for them. Writing a policy that addresses all 34 items of the TAGPEC but cannot be implemented because it is not feasible will do nothing to support children, families, or program staff. While we will discuss this more in the next chapter, we want to emphasize that our model represents a process rather than a final product, and, as stated in essential feature 7, a key feature of our model is continuous improvement.

CHAPTER 3

An Overview of the Five-Step Process

This chapter introduces the TAGPEC's five-step process as it is used in early childhood–education settings. Since writing our book *Effective Discipline Policies* (Longstreth and Garrity, 2018), we have continued to consult with program leaders on program-wide goals related to behavior-guidance policies, school climate, professional development, and data collection. In this chapter, we summarize each of the five steps and include examples from our work with a variety of early childhood programs.

We find it useful to think of the steps as a roadmap for working through issues at the program or systems level. They can also serve as a process to guide programs that are invested in implementing humanistic, anti-racist behavior-guidance practices that put an end to punitive discipline practices that further racial disparities in education. At the same time, we have seen that, because each program is unique, it is equally important for us to remain flexible to the needs, pace, and realities of each program. The goals and strategies described in this guidebook are aspirational and may not be feasible for some programs due to limitations of funding or existing policies. However, programs should find it encouraging that the approaches have been successfully implemented in programs throughout San Diego County, California. (We discuss some examples later in this chapter.) The steps are not linear but rather can be addressed according to the priorities of the program.

Importantly, we have found that investing in ongoing relationship building with the program leader is essential, regardless of the order in which the steps are accomplished. Program leaders, like the children, families, and staff that they serve, need a safe space for sharing the challenges and rewards of their work. (Chapter 5 of this guidebook provides a useful framework for how consultants can support this process.) A reminder: We use the term *consultant* to refer to the individual who is leading the efforts to assess and revise behavior-guidance policies using the TAGPEC five-step process. A consultant can also be a quality-improvement coach, the center or program director, a principal, or any other leader in the field. Because the TAGPEC five-step process focuses on the whole program, the consultant works primarily with the program leader (typically the program director or principal) to examine existing policies and practices around behavior guidance, identify program strengths as well as areas for improvement, and address issues related to the program's philosophy and policies and practices on behavior guidance. The goal of the TAGPEC five-step process is to build the capacity of the program leader and staff to support children's healthy social-emotional development and address challenging behaviors equitably and consistently.

This chapter also provides examples of how we have used our model to work with a range of early childhood programs and will hopefully highlight the versatility of the TAGPEC and how it is used to address a variety of program needs.

The TAGPEC Five-Step Process

It is Marina's second year as principal at a large elementary school located in a low-income, urban community. In addition to her role as principal of grades K–5, she is responsible for her school's state preschool program, which has three full-day classrooms serving children ages three to five years. Marina received some professional development on the importance of early childhood education, and her school district has recently begun exploring how to break down the silos between preschool and elementary classrooms and embrace a preschool-to-third grade approach to early childhood education. In addition, the school district just released a new discipline policy for all children, but Marina is concerned that it doesn't really reflect the needs of her youngest students. Marina's superintendent has arranged for a consultant to work with all new principals in the district, and Marina hopes to receive support on these issues

STEP 1: ASSEMBLE YOUR BEHAVIOR-GUIDANCE TEAM

The consultant meets with Marina to discuss the plan for the year. Marina shares her concern that many teachers at the school have experienced several different principals over the years. "They had a hard time accepting new leadership, and that was understandable," she explains. "Coming in, I wanted them to know I supported them, yet I also wanted to hold them accountable for supporting children's positive behavior (not just responding to negative behavior). Involving them in the creation of a new behavior-guidance policy will be an important way to show them that I want their feedback and buy-in."

The consultant notes Marina's commitment to creating a positive school climate for everyone and her willingness to invest in building relationships with the teachers. They discuss who might be important to include on the team and whose insight would need to be considered along the way. They also develop a plan for regular meetings and establish a date for finalizing the revised policy.

In the first step of TAGPEC process, the consultant contacts the program leader, describes the purpose of the consultation, and asks them to identify members of their behavior-guidance team. This team generally includes administrators, teachers, supervisors, support staff, parents, and early childhood mental-health and early-intervention staff. The goal at this step is to clarify expectations about the consultation and to discuss priorities.

The consultant approaches the program leader as the expert on the existing program and offers a supportive stance. In this role, the consultant begins to identify the leader's priorities for the TAGPEC five-step process. Besides developing or revising behavior-guidance policies, these goals may include improving the overall program climate, improving staff morale and wellness, increasing family engagement, and examining and refining professional-development practices.

STEP 2: COMMIT TO IMPROVING YOUR BEHAVIOR-GUIDANCE POLICY AND PRACTICE

Marina and the program consultant schedule a meeting with the team to discuss the plan and hear their perspectives. The team members include the school counselor, educational specialist, special-education preschool teacher, a third-grade teacher, and a paraprofessional. During the meeting, the consultant uses interview questions on the strengths, needs, and goals of the program to help the team reflect on what they perceive to be their strengths for supporting children's social-emotional well-being and what they see as challenges.

The preschool teacher notes that the school had some previous training on positive behavior support for working with children with special needs, but she believes that having more of this training could benefit all the children. The counselor comments that she feels very supported by the principal but often struggles when children who exhibit misbehaviors are sent to her office without the teacher first having tried the strategies the counselor has suggested. Marina shares that she sees the teachers as incredibly committed to their work and she wants to find ways to offer them as much support as possible. She does have concerns about the lack of accountability when it comes to processes related to behavior guidance, however, and wants to make sure that procedures are followed with more integrity and consistency.

During the second step of the process, the consultant meets with the team to learn about their perspectives. To facilitate this, the consultant can use the strengths, needs, and goals interview questions, which we developed to help the consultant learn more about the program and help the behavior-guidance team to develop broad goals for programmatic change. Program goals are general statements about what the program intends to accomplish. At the beginning of the consultation, the following questions can help guide the program administrator and the behavior-guidance team in developing broad goals for programmatic change. The team can revise the goals from time to time to meet the needs of the staff, children, and families.

The aim is to build a collaborative, mutual relationship in which the leader and staff feel that their perspectives, strengths, and goals are valued. Through reflective listening, the consultant works with the team to identify potential goals or areas of focus. The consultant can then reflect these goals back to the team and help them commit to working on these goals.

STEP 3: COLLECT THE PROGRAM GUIDANCE POLICY AND PRACTICE DOCUMENTS

Marina and her team compile all the program-level electronic documents related to social-emotional support and school discipline. For them, this included the school's existing discipline policy, the new discipline policy recently provided by the school district, staff and family handbooks, and the counselor's discipline referral form. The consultant scans and organizes the documents, then uploads them onto a Google Drive where all members of the team can access them.

The third step in the process is for programs to collect all existing information related to behavior guidance. While many programs have a stand-alone behavior-guidance or discipline policy, information about behavior-guidance policies and practices is often found in other documents, including family and staff handbooks, incident reports, behavior-support plan and referral forms, curriculum guides, and licensing documents. A critical part of revising a behavior-guidance policy is making sure that all documents are in alignment and reflect the program's philosophy, approach to behavior guidance, and goals.

STEP 4: ASSESS THE QUALITY OF THE PROGRAM'S EXISTING BEHAVIOR-GUIDANCE POLICY USING THE TAGPEC

Each team member is provided with a copy of the TAGPEC and asked to review and rate their policy using all the documents collected in the Google Drive. The consultant reminds team members that the intention of completing the TAGPEC is not to evaluate the program but to identify where the policies are strong and where they could be improved to be more equitable and inclusive.

The team meets again after two weeks to review their findings. Using the Behavior-Guidance Policy Action Plan Template (see appendix B) as her guide, the consultant identifies several strengths, including an emphasis in the policy on teaching children positive social-emotional skills. She also identifies several areas where the policy needs further elaboration or revision: clear and consistent program-wide behavior expectations, discussion of a three-tiered intervention for behavior support, and the implementation of staff training and data collection on disciplinary procedures.

The team discusses initial ideas for language, which the consultant notes. The consultant then creates a new document in the shared Google Drive with the revised policy. She adds in the draft language and invites all members of the team to contribute to the document.

The TAGPEC is a useful tool for helping programs to align to their goals. Ideally, each team member will complete it, but it can also be completed by the consultant and program leader if time is limited. Once everyone has completed the tool, the team comes together again to discuss their findings and to create an action plan. On our website (https://education.sdsu.edu/tagpec) we offer a free and easy-to-use training that shows how to administer and score the TAGPEC.

Next, the team identifies items from the TAGPEC that need additional attention and develops an action plan to address those items. Examples of this may include improving school climate, increasing staff and/or family satisfaction and wellness, or obtaining additional input from key stakeholders such as children and families. The consultant works with the behavior-guidance team to identify the areas of their policy that are strengths as well as areas that either aren't addressed in the policy or are outdated.

The consultant continues to serve as a support by asking for input on language to include in the policy. Sharing a document via a documentation collaboration tool, such as Google Drive or SharePoint, is useful for facilitating this process. Additionally, the consultant helps the team identify any gaps in the data and possible methods for collecting additional data, if needed.

STEP 5: IMPLEMENT AND MONITOR THE PROGRAM'S ACTION PLAN TO IMPROVE ITS BEHAVIOR-GUIDANCE POLICY

After consolidating feedback from the team, the consultant creates a final behavior-guidance policy and shares it with Marina and the team. They decide to share the new policy at the first professional-development training at the start of the new school year. The consultant will provide the training, and the principal and other members of the team will support the staff during small-group work.

A month later, they provide a second training to discuss the staff's experience in implementing the policy and to work out remaining questions and/or concerns. The team decides to meet three times per year to review their data and to revise the policy as needed.

In the final step of the TAGPEC program model, the team agrees on final versions of the behavior-guidance policy and any associated documents, such as referral forms and handbooks with discipline information. At this point, the consultant supports the program leader in communicating the new policy to staff, families, and children.

In our work implementing this model, we typically provide two professional-development workshops for staff; these workshops are individualized to meet the needs of the program. Often, the program leader wishes to use these workshops as opportunities to train the staff on the new policy. In other cases, the leader may wish to provide policy trainings and have the consultant supplement this with trainings on specialized topics related to social-emotional well-being, such as trauma-informed care or restorative justice. The specific topics can be arranged between the program leader and the consultant. Additionally, the consultant may provide the program leader with simple data-collection tools or procedures to ensure that the policy is being implemented effectively. For example, the team can agree to meet three times a year to review the policy, a school-climate survey, satisfaction scales, and discipline data to determine whether the policy is working and what changes might be needed.

As demonstrated by the experience of Marina and her team, the TAGPEC and related five-step process is effective for working alongside program leaders to promote children's healthy social-emotional development. The goal of program consultation is to build the capacity of the program leader by supporting and enhancing their ability to create a positive program climate. The tool and association worksheets can facilitate meaningful conversations between program leaders and staff so they are engaged in the process and in the outcomes. In the chapter 4, we describe how taking a consultative stance, rather than that of an expert, can be key to building trust and long-lasting change.

Using the TAGPEC and the Five-Step Process in a Variety of Settings

We have used the TAGPEC in a variety of early childhood settings, and this guidebook reflects the many lessons we have learned working with a wide variety of programs. In this section, we provide an overview of how we have used our model as part of our work in early childhood mental-health consultation, technical assistance and coaching, and quality-improvement coaching.

After reviewing the district's policy for restorative justice, the team determined that including a Restorative Response Matrix would ensure that staff had clear direction on how to address behaviors effectively. As a team, they developed a three-tier matrix that included developmentally appropriate supportive practices and responses for each tier of student behavior. At the time of this writing, the school is implementing the revised policy and matrix and collecting data on key indicators of progress, such as the number of office referrals, detentions, and suspensions.

● ● ● ● ●

Located in the city of El Cajon in San Diego County and serving approximately five hundred children, the El Cajon school district's early childhood program includes twenty-one preschool classrooms located across twelve schools. The program does not have site directors; instead, an early childhood director administers the program and is responsible for early intervention programs and transitional kindergarten as well. This project demonstrates the intersection of ECMHC and continuous quality-improvement efforts such as the Quality Rating and Improvement System (QRIS).

In 2019, the California Department of Education provided funds for implementing center-based ECMHC in subsidized child-care programs. The local county office of education partnered with First 5 California, a statewide agency committed to improving the lives of California's young children and families, to provide supplemental funds to support this pilot project. To qualify for participation, programs had to be part of QRIS and have a rating of 4 or 5 on the state's five-tiered rating system. An additional requirement was participation, through QRIS, in California's Teaching Pyramid Framework training, which is a series of five modules that address the key components of the Pyramid Model. These requirements are important, given that the Georgetown model cites the importance of a program's or school's readiness for consultation. We sought programs that had existing quality indicators in place, including administrative systems that could support ECMHC. The review of documents (Step 3) and the assessment of these documents using the TAGPEC (Step 4) indicated strong systems and policies in place, so the focus of consultation centered on the following:

- Making sure the behavior-guidance policy was consistent with all other documents

- Including explicit language in the policy about the strategies described by the Teaching Pyramid

- Expanding on third-tier strategies (Essential Feature 4, Item 23) by developing a process for student study teams (SSTs) in preschool classrooms

SSTs are used in elementary school settings to examine a student's academic, behavioral, and social-emotional progress and to propose interventions for the student. By implementing SSTs in both preschool and elementary settings, the program was able to strengthen the continuum between preschool and elementary schools and help ensure smooth transitions for children and families.

TECHNICAL ASSISTANCE AND COACHING

Coaches and technical-assistance providers have used the TAGPEC to improve the quality of their behavior-guidance policies and address issues related to suspension and expulsion in the early years. In the projects described below, Sarah and Sascha did not serve as consultants but supported coaches and other technical-assistance providers in using the TAGPEC and the related five-step program model.

Child Care Resources, located in Seattle, Washington, has used the TAGPEC to address their state's requirement that child-care providers have a no-expulsion policy. Program leaders decided to conduct a pilot program using the TAGPEC, which began with Sarah and Sascha providing training to early learning coaches. Following the training, the program invited early childhood programs to participate in a pilot, letting them know that they were seeking programs that had expelled, or were concerned about expelling, children because of challenging behavior. They also sought to work with programs that use so-called "soft suspensions"—removing a child from a play area, keeping a child inside during outdoor play, sending a child to the director's office, and so on—or those that had referred children for services because of challenging behavior prior to partnering with families and/or implementing other intervention strategies. Coaches worked with the participating early childhood programs using the TAGPEC and its five-step process. They met regularly with program staff to review behavior-guidance policies using the TAGPEC to identify which items from the tool were either present, emerging, or not present. Coaches supported program staff in setting goals related to crafting new behavior-guidance policies or refining existing policies. Using those goals, coaches supported program staff in developing behavior-guidance polices aligned with the TAGPEC items.

Providers who participated in the TAGPEC pilot were also given resources needed to support ongoing implementation of their behavior-guidance policies as well as resources to provide ongoing professional development for staff. The resources purchased included classroom materials that support social-emotional development and books to establish a resource library for staff and children in the program.

Feedback collected from coaches at the end of the pilot highlights the value of the TAGPEC five-step process. The following is feedback from one coach.

When the team first set out on creating this project to help programs revise their policies using the TAGPEC tool I felt intrigued and excited. Helping to create more equitable learning environments and dismantle the preschool to prison pipeline are both of great importance to me. Starting off a great deal of my focus was on how we are going to limit expulsions in programs and how can we create policies that support this goal. I did not however think about how programs view the purpose and use of their policies. In working with programs during this pilot I began to see how many programs constructed their policies as a safeguard to dismiss them from any liability. While I understand why protecting an organization legally is important and a pertinent step to ensuring its longevity it highlighted that in many policies the welfare of the child and family was not the focal point. The mentor sessions and group discussions during this pilot enable us all to dream of what a program policy could be and how it could serve all parties. This experience has helped me discover views and bias that though sometimes unintentional, can hinder us from investing in more equitable systems of conduct. The TAGPEC tool allowed us to dissect policies and examine them more critically. As this work continues, I hope that we will see more positive outcomes for both programs AND families as a result of these revisions.

Using the TAGPEC, we had deep, reflective conversations about behavior-guidance policies. We discussed using language that supports children's social-emotional development and emphasizes partnering with families and promoting strength-based, anti-racist implementation practices. This work is ongoing. We continue to meet weekly with side-by-side coaching as the director incorporates each of the TAGPEC seven essential features into the program's behavior-guidance policy. A next step in coaching at this site is having a book study using *Don't Look Away: Embracing Anti-Bias Classrooms* (Iruka, Curenton, Durden, and Escayg, 2020). The TAGPEC pilot allowed for the reflective space needed to think through behavior-guidance policies with an anti-racist lens.

• • • • •

We have also worked with a statewide project in Wisconsin through the Wisconsin Alliance for Infant Mental Health that has used the TAPGEC to guide technical assistance in policy development aimed at reducing and eliminating the suspension and expulsion of infants, toddlers, and young children. Regional cross-sector professional-development provider teams have used the TAGPEC to independently review policies and then share and discuss scores. These cross-sector teams represent Wisconsin's structure for providing training and technical assistance to universal pre-K and early childhood special education, child-care programs, and Pyramid Model programs. The goal of this work is to consider the feasibility, utility, and efficiency of using the TAGPEC and the five-step model to help facilitate community conversations about current policy and practices related to behavior guidance, suspension, and expulsion.

The aim of this chapter is to provide an overview of the TAGPEC five-step process and share concrete examples of how it can be used in a variety of settings. The next chapter describes the consultative stance that is essential to this process.

CHAPTER 4

The Consultative Stance

Children do not exist in a vacuum, and the contextual nature of child development is key to our humanistic approach to behavior guidance. You are most likely reading this guidebook because you recognize the importance of high-quality early childhood environments and the critical need to support those who care for young children—essentials that play pivotal roles in a child's development and social and academic success.

Supporting the early childhood workforce and providing high-quality early childhood programming is difficult, especially when faced with children's challenging behaviors and issues related to discipline and behavior guidance. That is why many, including the authors of the TAGPEC, have used terms such as *behavior guidance* in lieu of *discipline*. However, it is important to understand the relationship we might have with the words we hear when challenging behaviors arise, terms such as *discipline* or *punishment* and derogatory terms such as *bad*, *lazy*, or *manipulative*.

In adults, children's challenging behavior often leads to strong feelings and beliefs, which are often rooted in our own upbringing and culture. How we, as consultants, coaches, and early childhood leaders, respond to these big feelings and beliefs (both ours and those of others) can dramatically influence the success or failure of program consultation. Our own histories, experiences, and backgrounds can cause us to overidentify with certain groups. For example, Sarah's experience as a program director for a Head Start program often causes her to overidentify with the program directors she works with and not always consider how the teachers may feel. My (Lisa's) background working directly with children and families drives me to advocate for the child. Challenging behaviors may also activate our protective instincts and desire to advocate or defend those who are vulnerable in the system. Without consciously understanding and harnessing these instincts and drives, we can alienate members of the behavior-guidance team and ultimately restrict the important work we are trying to do.

The Reflective Framework

In this chapter, we discuss an approach that can be helpful in managing the challenging conversations that may arise when implementing the TAGPEC and its five-step model. In many fields, the position of a consultant is typically that of an expert who is there to impart crucial information and/or make important changes to an agency, person, or environment. However, in the context of both the TAGPEC program consultation model and early childhood mental health consultation, we are not acting in the position of the expert. Although we use our expertise to guide programs, administrators, and their staff through the five-step process, we operate as a partner and collaborator and offer support as we work through the process with behavior-guidance teams.

Our goal is to create a space within which the program can align its values and philosophies with best practices and develop actionable steps to support children's social-emotional development equitably. The role of the program consultant is to create a reflective space, engage as a partner and not an expert, and maintain a curious approach to interactions while hearing and integrating the perspectives and challenges each stakeholder is bringing to the organization. At the same time, the consultant must manage their own biases, monitor their emotional triggers, and regulate their own emotions. This can be challenging when discussing behavior guidance, as so many of our own values and beliefs are grounded in our own experiences and beliefs about what children need to succeed.

To engage in this type of consultation, we assert that the consultant must simultaneously hold in mind their own and the consultees' experiences and behaviors. One of the most effective ways to manage all these perspectives is through reflective practice, for both the consultant and the program staff. In this section, we describe the central components of the reflective framework that can be used by consultants to facilitate change. To support ongoing reflective practice and demonstrate how the consultative staff can be integrated in our model, we will provide exercises called "Pause to Reflect" to help you use reflection in each step of our process.

SELF-REFLECTION

Reflection allows a space for stepping back from the immediate work (psychologically in the moment or physically after a situation has passed) to assess all the perspectives in the work, how those perspectives may affect the work, and how to improve the efficacy of work while considering all perspectives involved. This serves as a core feature of program consultation and is twofold. First, the consultant must reflect on their own standing, position, experience, and challenges so they can hold, without bias, the perspective of all those involved in the program consultation. This is done through an ongoing and shared practice of self-reflection. Sounds easy right? Let's practice. Read the "Pause to Reflect" section and don't move on until you have formed the answers to the questions in that section.

PAUSE TO REFLECT

Take a minute to think about a time when you felt that you were held back from something or a time when your work was harder because of a rule that did not make sense—"red tape" that seemed pointless and endless. Was there a time when someone in power held your fate in their hands and whose authority could make your life easier or harder? Do you have the image in your head? Great! Now how did you feel? Then, what did you do? Looking back, would you do anything differently?

Do you have unresolved feelings about that situation? Did you feel victimized? Or did you feel empowered to speak up? Maybe you felt angry. Maybe you felt helpless. Maybe you advocated for yourself, or maybe you walked away from the whole situation. Your response to this situation was likely driven by your background and experiences as well as your sense of safety, positionality, and agency within that situation. How this situation was resolved or not resolved can also affect your internal response when others you are working with face similar situations.

We use this example specifically because the conflict between policy and practice is a common tension within program consultation. Each stakeholder group holds its own tension and conflict around these topics, which touch on deeply rooted histories and vulnerable feelings of powerlessness. Administrators are often at the mercy of licensing and other bureaucratic requirements, including employment laws and/or union limitations, and funding is always a concern. Teachers often have little say in administrator decisions yet are responsible for child safety, curriculum implementation, and assessment, and for fulfilling a myriad of other requirements intended to support children's growth and development that become more difficult to accomplish when faced with children's challenging behavior. Families may feel they have little say in what goes on at the center or that they only hear from program staff when something is wrong. Families may feel threatened by the potential of suspension and/or expulsion and may worry how this will affect them economically. Each of these groups may be having similar experiences yet feel extremely isolated. How these feelings are (or are not) discussed, addressed, and responded to sets a precedent, and left unattended they will shape the culture of the program. This brings us to the second aspect of the reflective framework that is crucial to program consultation: reflective facilitation.

REFLECTIVE FACILITATION

Holding a reflective space for the behavior-guidance team is the context within which the five steps of our model unfold and begin the change-making process. It sounds magical, and it is! But all wands aside, the consultant's role here is not to just hold all perspectives but also to begin to build the perspective-taking capacity of the behavior-guidance team as they assess how the behavior-guidance policies and practices may affect the stakeholders, such as children of color or children with a disability, in different ways.

Broadly, *reflective facilitation* "builds the capacity of individuals, relationships, and organizations by cherishing strengths and partnering around vulnerabilities" (Shahmoon-Shanok, 1991). Reflective facilitation within TAGPEC and its five-step program consultation model builds the capacity of individuals working with and for young children to proactively consider the implications of policies for those involved and to notice any reactivity within the behavior-guidance team. This reactivity may arise from entrenched beliefs about children or authority, implicit biases, or their own history of trauma that is triggered by challenging behaviors. The consultant must then help regulate thoughts, actions, and words to reach the best outcome for children and ensure that policies reflect best practices that establish equitable, developmentally appropriate, and predictable responses to children's challenging behavior.

Let's look at an example.

> During the pandemic workforce shortage, early childhood classrooms everywhere were struggling to maintain teacher-child ratios. One program we worked with continually struggled with this issue, and teachers felt that although they continually asked for help during staff meetings, they never received a response from the administration. A teacher finally told the program administrator that she needed a substitute in her classroom. The administrator, feeling overwhelmed by juggling so many responsibilities, laughed in the teacher's face. Understandably, the teacher felt hurt, disrespected, and worried about the safety of the children in her classroom. The consultant met with the administrator to highlight the importance of allocating resources to this problem given the licensing-compliance issues. During and after this meeting, the administrator became defensive and difficult to contact. The teacher later filed a complaint with human resources about feeling unheard and disrespected by the administrator.

PAUSE TO REFLECT

What came up for you when reading this vignette? What emotions, thoughts, problem-solving ideas, and so on did you have? Who did you feel the strongest empathy for and/or identify with the most? The answers to these questions may highlight tendencies to overidentify with certain groups within the early childhood workforce and also may highlight the importance of reflective practice as a consultant. When you are around strong emotions, how do you feel inside? When you identify a problem, is your first response to begin problem solving?

As you begin to think about what you might do in this situation, we encourage you to stop. Yes, you read that right! Stop. One of the most important parts of reflective facilitation is the capacity of the facilitator to do the work *with* rather than *for* the team. You most likely entered this field because you want to help people, a desire that may often lead you (like us) to solve a problem right away.

> Prior to becoming a professor, Sarah spent many years as an administrator for a Head Start program. She juggled multiple demands each day, including ensuring compliance with state and federal regulations designed to ensure quality programming for children and families, ensuring licensing requirements were met, and the day-to-day issues that come up when caring for young children (for example, teacher-child ratios, making sure meals get delivered and the bus is on time, and so on). Because she is so familiar with the demands of early childhood programs, she often finds herself over-identifying with very busy program directors. In one instance, upon reflection, she realized that she did too much of the work for a behavior-guidance team because she wanted to take

something off their very full plate. Because of this, she rushed through Step 2: Commit to improving your behavior-guidance policy and practice. Thus, she did not support the team in engaging in the deep reflection and dialogue that is needed to clarify goals, values, and beliefs related to discipline and behavior guidance. She also skipped through some of the important features of Step 4: Assess the quality of your behavior-guidance plan, and did not complete the Behavior-Guidance Policy Action Plan with the team but instead went straight to writing the policy. In doing so, she missed an important step intended to ensure that goals for the behavior-guidance policy are realistic and reflect the values of the team.

We don't know about you, but we were already headed to our cars to get our capes about three sentences into that story and had about a million practical solutions to the problem. Because we (Sarah, Sascha, and Lisa) have roles as administrators, we are used to people coming to us to solve problems and give them the answers. It takes a conscious effort to step back in our role as consultants and remember the power of creating spaces where multiple perspectives can be acknowledged and explored as part of the reflective process.

In the vignette above, the consultants focused on addressing the problem with the administrator. In reflecting on that experience, we notice that focusing on the problem didn't work. The alliance and collaborative relationship that had been formed with the administrator during the consultation process fell apart in the wake of problem solving. How many times have your awesome suggestions been rejected by the very people you think need them the most? We often forget or lose sight of the real people behind the problem and fail to consider multiple perspectives.

Let's consider the multiple perspectives in the vignette described above:

- The licensing requirements that are in place to keep children safe

- The perspectives of a very stressed administrator (who does want to keep children safe)

- The perspectives of a very stressed teacher (who also wants to keep children safe)

- The context of a worldwide pandemic that has stretched the already very underresourced early childhood sector to the brink

The administrator had, unbeknownst to the teacher and consultant, been trying desperately to navigate the workforce shortage, had expended all available resources in looking for a substitute without success, and had been contacting the school-district leadership with increasingly desperate demands for help. We, as consultants, missed an opportunity for connection, to hear the administrator's experiences and give voice to the vulnerability of someone who was feeling unable to protect the staff and children an administrator is responsible for. Our own activation and protective instincts rallied around the problem rather than the person. Yet another case for self-reflection as a crucial tool in the consultant's toolbox!

It is essential that those engaging in consultation at the program level be aware of their own emotional activation and tendencies for rescuing so they can hold a space for others. Only then can the behavior-guidance team begin to discuss difficult topics, make decisions, and explore the implications of those decisions. Our own regulation is crucial for the regulation of our consultees. When we are regulated, we are better able to provide the safe, open, and nonjudgmental relationship, often called the "relationship for learning" (Shahmoon-Shanok, 2006). You may have heard that we learn from experience; this is a widely held misconception. Experience is, in fact, the touchpoint of events rather than the integration of knowledge. It is the act of reflecting on experience that allows us to place the touchpoint in context with our worldview and experiences. Reflection creates meaning from experience. So how do we begin to create the relationship for learning? We circle back to first understanding the person and their perspective. Let's try it. Pause to reflect, and don't move on until you have a guess or two.

PAUSE TO REFLECT

Think for a moment. How might you communicate to the administrator that you genuinely seek to understand them and their experience of the problem?

We might start from a place of curiosity and empathy. We might display curiosity by asking, for example, "How are you coping with the stress of the ratio issue?" When we are under stress, our capacity for reason and problem solving is diminished, if not completely offline. If we can first connect to the very real person behind the problem (the administrator, in this case), they will not only feel safe to explore the vulnerable aspects of their position, but this approach will provide them with the space to reengage the parts of their brain that were quite literally pushed out of the way when their survival instincts took over and they laughed at the teacher's request.

The administrator's laughter arose from their own sense of helplessness and from feeling overwhelmed by a lack of resources and the many expectations placed upon them by the state, the school district, teachers, students, staff, and parents. Similarly, the teacher felt underresourced, unable to manage the classroom, and unable to get the help she needed. This likely trickled down to the children in the classroom, increasing stress and decreasing the emotional safety in the classroom. Drawing parallels across all three of these levels may help the early childhood program staff begin to build their capacity to connect with one another in times of stress, thus ensuring that they are more emotionally available to the children in their care. With connection comes empathy. If we wonder with the administrator over "What a challenging position everyone is in," or reflect back, "It sounds like you are both in an impossible situation," we begin to draw a connection between the two groups (administrators and teachers), where previously they were adversaries. Highlighting these similarities, often called the *parallel processes*, are a core feature of reflective facilitation and can serve to zoom perspectives in or out and build empathy.

The reflective framework, including both self-reflection and facilitating reflection, serves as a potential foundation for consultants when navigating the complexities of programmatic consultation. This chapter represents only a small window into reflective capacity building in yourself and your consultees. We urge you to further this exploration through many of the resources listed on page 88 and to return to this chapter when you feel things getting a little bit wobbly in your consultation. Additionally, we encourage you to take the time to do the reflection pauses throughout the rest of this guidebook, as this will continue to support you on your journey as you make meaning out of experience for both yourself and your consultees.

2

Part Two

Improving Your
Behavior-Guidance Policy
Using the TAGPEC

CHAPTER 5

Step 1: Assemble Your Behavior-Guidance Team

In this section, we take a closer look at the process of implementing the TAGPEC's five-step program consultation model in early childhood education settings. As we describe in the introduction, the process of crafting and fully implementing a high-quality behavior-guidance policy often takes three to five years. In this sense, the steps that we present in this guidebook are more cyclical than linear, and we expect programs will engage in the steps multiple times before a true shift in the program discipline culture occurs. This guidebook is intended as a resource for programs to use repeatedly as they move through the cyclical process.

As described briefly in chapter 2, in the first step, the consultant contacts the program administrator to describe the purpose of the programmatic consultation and to request that the administrator begin to identify potential team members. During this initial phone call or meeting, the consultant can help the administrator understand that creating high-quality guidance policies and practices is not something they can do on their own. Rather, the process is deeply collaborative and therefore involves shared decision-making between the administrator and other team members. The advantage to this approach is that staff are likely to feel more committed to the guidance policy when they have had an opportunity to be involved in its development. At the same time, the consultant can emphasize the critical role of the administrator in leading and motivating the team through the consultation process. In particular, the consultant can encourage the administrator to empower team and staff members to provide input into the planning process.

Making Plans

Implementing Plans

Monitoring

Evaluation

Learning from Experience

In many programs, the members of the behavior-guidance team generally include administrators, educators, student-support professionals, and early childhood mental-health and early intervention staff. On several occasions, we have worked with programs that have included a student's parent on the team. Parents can be helpful in expanding the consultant's understanding of the context of the program and the interrelationships across environments. Involving parents can also help create a significant link among the primary settings in a child's life: the home, early childhood program, and community environments. Parent involvement helps to promote the sustainability of the intervention over time and across settings.

The Role of the Administrator

The administrator plays a critical role in leading the team through the planning and implementation process. The following list summarizes the primary responsibilities of the administrator in programmatic consultation.

- Ensuring that all staff understand humanistic behavior-guidance policies and practices and why these policies and practices are being implemented

- Establishing a commitment to anti-racist and equitable behavior-guidance policies and practices

- Identifying existing strengths in programs on the use of guidance and incorporating those strengths into the behavior-guidance policy

- Communicating with students, families, and the community about the policy and the need to implement humanistic behavior-guidance practices in the program

- Assembling a behavior-guidance team that can commit to the ongoing process of designing and implementing a humanistic behavior-guidance policy

- Organizing professional-development trainings for all staff to prepare them to be successful in implementing the policy

- Establishing ongoing communication with the team to monitor, evaluate, and revise as needed the implementation of the policy

We have found that most administrators agree readily to this list of items and that they want to have unbiased and supportive discipline policies. In fact, you would be hard-pressed to find someone actively working with children who would not agree. Additionally, many administrators may feel they already fulfill these roles and responsibilities. Here, we must employ a more reflective stance that encourages greater depth of discussion around the administrator's own history, experiences, knowledge, and beliefs surrounding discipline. Administrators should have or be willing to work toward a strong belief in humanistic, anti-racist behavior-guidance policies and practices and a readiness to hold others accountable throughout the planning and implementation process. The work of committing to anti-racism is challenging and often emotional. As author Bettina Love describes it, "Too often we think the work of fighting oppression is just intellectual. The real work is personal, emotional, spiritual, and communal" (Love, 2019). In other words, implementing anti-racist policies and practices requires administrators and staff to honestly examine their own racial identities, their ideas about race, and how their ideas affect students of color. Following are some Pause to Reflect questions that can assist you, as an administrator, in assessing your readiness to engage in anti-racist work.

PAUSE TO REFLECT

As an administrator, think about the role that race plays in your program's discipline practices. Ask yourself the following questions, and answer as honestly as possible:

1. Have I examined my own racial identity and my positionality when it comes to engaging in anti-racist work? How can I grow?

2. Do I accept that race and racism are embedded in our society and have impacted how children are disciplined on a systematic level?

3. How do I talk about race to my staff and the families we serve? Am I listening as well as sharing?

4. How can I use my privilege as a school administrator to stand up against racial injustice and racial inequity when it comes to discipline in my program?

These questions may arise frequently as you engage in planning with your team. It's important for everyone on the team to feel they have an opportunity to reflect and discuss their beliefs about anti-racism, and this can occur during an initial meeting and/or as an ongoing conversation. It is worth noting that the administrator has a particular responsibility to help create a sense of safety within the team. Work regarding discipline is especially sensitive given that everyone brings their own experiences, beliefs, and identities to the table. Part of the role of the administrator is to establish ground rules for communicating ideas, even when those ideas are not in agreement with those of the larger group. For example, teachers may not agree about how to discipline a child who acted aggressively toward another child who used a racial slur against her. It is critical that the administrator allow staff to share multiple perspectives but at the same time remind the team of the goal of promoting equitable discipline.

The Role of the Consultant

A consultant can be someone from outside the program, a quality-improvement coach, a center or program director, a principal, or any other leader in the field. As with the other team members, the role of the consultant is collaborative rather than authoritative. We see the consultant as more of a facilitator than as an expert. Each program is unique, and while the consultant may have a broad knowledge of effective guidance strategies, it is the team members who know the program and their population best and can apply the strategies in meaningful and relevant ways. Therefore, the consultant approaches the administrator as the expert on their program and offers a supportive, reflective stance.

During the initial conversation, the consultant can explore the overall goal of the administrator for participating in the consultation. We've noticed that programs' goals vary widely depending on their specific context, strengths, and needs. For example, an administrator may want to focus on aligning the program guidance policy to the district policy (Linda Vista), on integrating program-specific values into the guidance policy (Dot to Dot), or on increasing staff morale and wellness and family engagement (Barrio Logan). The overall goal will be explored in greater depth when the team meets; at this stage, it is helpful just to get a sense of the administrator's primary motivation for engaging in the work.

Building the Team

The administrator compiles a list of potential team members, then contacts each person to determine their willingness to commit to the behavior-guidance implementation process. We encourage administrators to give team members, when possible, an opportunity to express any questions, concerns, or ideas regarding their involvement before committing to the process. The administrator then organizes an initial meeting with the team to share the purpose of the process and to establish expectations. This initial meeting is an ideal time for the administrator to create a safe space for the team to have honest conversations about discipline. To do this, the administrator can let the team know that they have permission to be honest, to ask questions at any time, and to express any concerns that they feel haven't been fully addressed. To help with this, the administrator can model asking permission of the team members with questions like, "May I ask you something?" or "May I play devil's advocate for a minute?" What is important is that each person feels as though they can fully express themselves, even if they disagree.

To create a space for honest conversations about discipline, the administrator will need to create a sense of psychological safety for everyone in the group. Each group member will have arrived with their own personal experiences of participating in groups, and most will have at least one previous experience in which they did not feel heard or validated. These experiences may be especially heightened for team members from minoritized groups, due to years of institutional racism, sexism, ableism, and other forms of discrimination. The administrator can help to create a safe psychological space by sharing or even co-creating some simple community agreements at the very first meeting. Examples of community agreements include aspects such as the following:

- Together, we know a lot. Alone, we don't know it all!

- Do your best. Be curious and respectful.

- Take space. Make space.

- Lean into discomfort. It's how we grow.

- Uphold what's confidential. What we learn leaves here. What we say stays here (Drawing Change, 2019).

Community agreements are useful to revisit at the start of every meeting as a reminder of the safety of the space as well as a reference point for when conflict arises. The administrator may initially take the lead on referencing the agreements, but over time, the hope is that the team members assume mutual responsibility for creating psychological safety within the group.

Respecting Confidentiality

Given the sensitive nature of the work, it's worth mentioning the agreement of confidentiality in more detail. Many children who have experienced disciplinary actions in programs have complex histories, and these histories can be reflected in the program data. For example, information about a child's family or medical history may arise during a team meeting, and this information may not be familiar to everyone at the table. Similarly, others may be hearing for the first time about a child's behavior incident reports, types of behavior, or lists of referrals that they have received. It is the administrator's responsibility to convey to the team the importance of confidentiality. One way that the administrator can articulate this is by saying that information shared in the group is sensitive, and sharing it with others (and out of context) could cause the child harm. The information, including any forms of data, are intended only to help the group learn and develop stronger policies and practices. The same can be said for anything shared by a team member; if team members are truly to feel a sense of safety, they need to know that their honesty will be protected by everyone at the table.

Establishing the Time Commitment

When the team has established community agreements, the administrator can move forward with discussing the logistics of the TAGPEC and the five-step process. Because there is a significant time commitment associated with the planning process, we suggest being as transparent as possible about the work expectations for the team. Typically, the various roles on a team are shared, so no one person will be responsible for all the work. Everyone on the team brings with them their own expertise and strengths, and these can be applied in the planning process. For example, the special-education preschool teacher at Linda Vista was instrumental in providing developmentally appropriate support responses for the behavior matrix. The school counselor was able to track data on office referrals, suspensions, and expulsions, which the team used to inform their decisions. It is important to establish a clear time commitment to this process. In our experience, the planning process takes approximately eight to twelve weeks, depending on how often the team meets. We recommend a series of four two-hour planning meetings in which all team members can be present. Given the impact of the COVID-19 pandemic in recent years, we have explored virtual meetings and have found that they can be an effective and convenient format for meeting on a regular basis. We suggest outlining the meetings with the corresponding goals in a table-format timeline or calendar; we have provided a sample timeline in appendix C. This type of timeline can be useful for the administrator when sharing expectations for workload and time commitment with the team.

Setting Roles and Responsibilities

At the first meeting with the team, the consultant introduces the goal of programmatic consultation and provides an overview of the tasks and timeline. It may be helpful at this point for the consultant to share a sample policy and timeline to provide the team members with a clear vision of the final outcome. During this meeting, the consultant also engages the team in a discussion about the various roles and responsibilities and how different team members can work together effectively. Worksheet 1 in appendix B provides a template that includes a list of possible roles and responsibilities with columns that can be filled in by the consultant or administrator. Throughout this process, the consultant emphasizes collaborative problem-solving. No one individual is considered an expert on *all* aspects of the program; rather, each team member brings a unique perspective that enhances the overall quality of the behavior-guidance policy.

As the team works to identify roles and responsibilities, the consultant may want to introduce the issue of mandated reporting. During one of my consultations with a program, I became aware of a licensing violation related to teacher-student ratios. The incident was unfortunately not an isolated occurrence but rather had come up frequently in conversations with the teachers. Because the issue presented safety problems for the children, I was mandated to report this to the program administrator. Unfortunately, my conversation with the administrator resulted in the team feeling judged and defensive, despite my efforts to share the incident as objectively as possible. In light of this experience, I spoke with my co-authors, and we discussed the need to be up front with administrators when beginning consultation about our responsibility as mandated reporters. As in therapeutic settings, we have adopted a simple document that acknowledges our role as mandated reporters that both the administrator and the consultant sign at the start of the consultation process. This document lets us be transparent about our obligation and role should a concern arise.

PAUSE TO REFLECT

You have assembled a planning team that consists of yourself, the administrator, one lead toddler teacher, one lead preschool teacher, a behavioral specialist, and a parent representative. At your first meeting, how might you develop a common understanding of what a "high-quality, equitable guidance policy" means? How might you help the team create an imagined future of what the program will be once the policy is developed and implemented? What questions might you ask the team to help them reflect on their priorities while also working toward the common goal?

Focusing on Strengths and Establishing Commitment

Once the logistics of the group and the roles have been established, the programmatic consultant begins the process of building a relationship with the team by engaging them in a dialogue about their strengths and needs. We've provided a list of possible questions in appendix B (Worksheet 2: Strengths, Needs, and Goals Interview Questions), but we encourage consultants to expand on these to fit the unique needs of a program. This dialogue can help the consultant elicit the team's understanding of their strengths and challenges and can assist in identifying focus points for the consultation. Throughout this process, the consultant should help the team focus on the program's competencies or strengths rather than on their deficits. By emphasizing a program's strengths, the consultant is validating their worth and ability to attain their unique goals, which is an extension of our humanistic approach to behavior guidance.

A program's readiness for change is one issue that often arises during this first step. *Readiness* refers to the program's degree of preparedness to engage in the design and implementation of a new initiative. Implementing new policies and practices around discipline sometimes brings up issues of personal beliefs and values for staff. Embarking on new initiatives can also sometimes feel overwhelming to staff who are deeply engaged in responding to students, families, and colleagues on a consistent basis. A program's willingness to be honest about their readiness depends on the consultant's approach. In our experience, we have identified at least three categories of readiness:

- **Administrator readiness:** To what extent is the program administrator ready to engage in using the TAGPEC and implementing the five-step process? What is their level of openness, self-awareness, and knowledge about discipline policies? Do they have the time necessary to commit to the process, or are there other priorities that take precedence?

- **Organizational readiness:** To what extent are resources available to support the administrator and staff in the process? Is there sufficient funding to support staff professional development and release time? Is there a system in place for sharing documents and providing feedback?

- **Staff readiness:** To what extent are staff ready to engage in the process? Are there other demands on their time that make authentic engagement in the process too challenging at this time? Do staff feel safe and supported by the administration in a way that will enable their honest participation in this work?

While some programs may be ready to design and implement all thirty-four items of the TAGPEC into their policy and practice, others may need to focus on specific items or sections of the TAGPEC to start. Consultants should approach each program with a proactive, positive, and nonjudgmental stance to facilitate open communication and a collaborative work environment. Rather than saying to an administrator, for example, "I don't think you are ready for this work," the consultant might say, "I see you have a lot of priorities at the moment, but I can also see that you are committed to this work. I wonder how we might carve out time once a month to work on this, even if it means extending the timeline a bit?"

By using this approach, the consultant can learn about the program's strengths and its barriers. Barriers might include, for example, time constraints for engaging in the process, a lack of time and/or funding for educator professional development on the policies, limited staff and/or educator buy-in, and insufficient administrator support. The consultant should, therefore, openly discuss potential barriers and determine how and whether they should be addressed.

We've provided reflective questions in appendix B (Worksheet 3: Behavior-Guidance Team Reflection Questions) to guide your conversations with the team about their readiness. These questions serve as a starting point for conversations about the behavior-guidance policy but can help the consultant to establish a stronger understanding of the program's existing commitment, resources, and limitations.

At the end of the first team meeting, we suggest asking the administrator to restate the purpose of implementing humanistic behavior-guidance policies and practices. The administrator must be clear about the expectation of humanistic guidance practices and must be unafraid to speak to racial disparities in school discipline. The administrator's belief and commitment to teaching positive social-emotional skills is critical to staff support and buy-in. A level of trust between the administrator and staff is especially important in this process, as administrators will be responsible for holding staff accountable for discipline practices that do not reflect the new model.

In summary, step 1 of programmatic consultation includes the following:

- The consultant meets with the program administrator to describe the purpose of the programmatic consultation and works with the administrator to identify potential members of their behavior-guidance team.

- Once the team is assembled, the consultant meets with them to discuss the purpose of programmatic consultation, the timeline, and the various roles and responsibilities.

- The team and the consultant explore the team's perspectives on existing program strengths and needs and their readiness to engage in implementation.

- Throughout this process, the consultant supports the program administrator in establishing their vision and commitment to the team.

- When the administrator and the team have expressed support for and a commitment to transforming the program's discipline policies to reflect a humanistic, instructive approach, they are ready for step 2.

CHAPTER 6

Step 2: Commit to Improving Your Behavior-Guidance Policy and Practice

The second step of the TAGPEC five-step process is to work with the team to revise or develop their existing commitment statement (sometimes referred to as a mission statement) so that it reflects the humanistic approach to behavior guidance. The behavior-guidance commitment statement may be a component of the program's overall mission statement, or it may be a separate statement dedicated specifically to discipline and behavior guidance. The consultant can describe the commitment statement as a roadmap that helps keep programs on track and working toward their shared goals. With a commitment statement in hand, it becomes easier for the team to persist through challenging situations, guide decision-making, inspire staff and families, and establish team commitment. Additionally, by having a clear set of shared values, the team has a foundation to return to throughout the process to assess whether they are making progress, and the consultant can use it as a reflective tool.

> **PAUSE TO REFLECT**
>
> What is your program's current commitment or mission statement? Does it currently reflect the goals and values of the program? Does it address your program's approach to discipline, either directly or indirectly? Does it embody a humanistic approach to discipline whereby each child is viewed as having the potential for self-actualization?

The commitment statement typically consists of two elements: a statement of purpose and a declaration of values. A statement of purpose expresses why the program has chosen to adopt a more equitable, inclusive, and humanistic discipline policy. The consultant can facilitate the team's writing of this statement by asking them what greater impact they hope to have on the children, educators, and families. The purpose will relate to the program's original goal for seeking consultation and working to improve the quality of discipline policies and practices.

The second element of a commitment statement is a declaration of values that connect to the team's beliefs about child guidance and discipline. Values set expectations for how staff engage with one another, with the children, and with the families. The declaration communicates what is important to the program and provides direction for decision-making. Some programs prefer to use the term *principles*; the terms can be used interchangeably. We've provided an example of a commitment statement in appendix B and a template with guiding questions for helping the team create their own commitment statement (worksheet 3).

Focusing on the spirit of growth and innovation is particularly helpful when working with a program on its mission statement. Ideally, programs will come to view themselves as stretching to meet new goals, so in this sense their mission is both aspirational and strategic. The focus on growth provides programs with a high-quality roadmap.

PAUSE TO REFLECT

- What is your imagined future for your program when it comes to behavior guidance?

- How does this imagined future align with your goal to engage in anti-racist guidance policies and practices?

It may be helpful here to think about your philosophical and theoretical approach to discipline and behavior guidance.

- What are your guiding beliefs about discipline?

- How might you get group consensus on your mission?

One way to approach this task is to ask your team to discuss the Team Reflection Questions on worksheet 3 in appendix B. These questions ask team members to think about their own discipline experiences, including the ways that culture played a role, and to consider how their experiences affect their interactions with students.

Ideally, the mission statement will be widely circulated and discussed among key stakeholders. Stakeholders are those individuals with some influence over the program or a stake in its future. This includes the staff, educators, children, and community or corporate sponsors. The more that all key stakeholders understand the program's mission and values, the more likely the mission statement will be widely understood and internalized.

At Dot to Dot preschool, for example, teachers and staff were asked to provide their insight into the values and mission during a hands-on workshop. The director presented the four general values. Then the consultant asked the teachers and staff to provide their thoughts, examples, and ideas about each value by writing them down on sticky notes and placing them around the room. A follow-up discussion revealed that the teachers and staff were deeply committed to these values and, through the exercise, were able to come to a shared language and understanding of the roles they played in the guidance policy. Students could also be involved in this process using similar hands-on strategies and through conversations in community circles.

We recognize that the process of communicating with stakeholders can be time-consuming and is, therefore, not always feasible. We've found it helpful to offer specific opportunities for families and community members to provide their input, such as an open meeting or email communication with a format for giving feedback, such as a Google form.

One strategy that can be helpful in implementing a new discipline model is to invite other administrators and/or staff from other programs that have implemented humanistic approaches to share their methods, successes, and challenges. This strategy works particularly well if stakeholders are resistant to implementing a model that is so different from the traditional approach to addressing children's behavioral challenges. A commitment to a new model will be most effective when data are used to support the need for a new approach and the school community can learn about and become invested in the new model.

✳ ✳ ✳

In summary, step 2 of the TAGPEC five-step process is to guide the team toward developing a mission statement that reflects the humanistic approach to behavior guidance. The mission statement, developed by the behavior-guidance team, serves as a roadmap for keeping programs on track as they work toward implementing discipline reform. There are two primary elements of the mission statement: the statement of purpose and the values declaration. The statement will continue to serve as a foundation for the program as they move forward with developing new guidance policies and practices.

CHAPTER 7

Step 3: Collect the Program Guidance Policy and Practice Documents

In the third step, the consultant works with the team to gather the program's existing documentation as it relates to behavior guidance and discipline. The goal of this step is to compile all relevant information so that an accurate self-assessment of the guidance policy can be made. At the conclusion of this step, the team members will have all of the information they need to independently assess the quality of the current policy using the TAGPEC.

The information in the documentation helps the team identify where the program's discipline philosophy, approach, strategies, and protocols are addressed. Each document will eventually need to reflect the program's new approach to behavior guidance, so it's important to be thorough at this stage. Although many programs have a stand-alone behavior-guidance or discipline policy, information about behavior-guidance policies and practices are often found in other documents as well, including family and staff handbooks, incident reports, behavior-support plan and referral forms, curriculum guides, licensing documents, and website content. This may mean considering data that you are already collecting but not necessarily using to guide your behavior-guidance practices.

As with the other steps in the process, the entire team's input is critical to ensuring that the program is comprehensive in its approach. For example, educators may have documentation about existing classroom expectations. The counselor may have records of referrals for discipline referrals and student-support professionals. Similarly, if there is a member of the team in special education, she may have information on the frequency and type of IFSPs/IEPs. If your program consults with outside partners or specialists to collect data, consider reaching out to them to determine whether they have data that could be useful. For example, Linda Vista had partnerships with the county juvenile justice commission and the district restorative-justice program, both of which had valuable data regarding students who had received school discipline.

Note that with all records that involve individual children, it is critical that the team only share that data in de-identified or aggregated (summarized) form. Information on specific students should be de-identified before it's shared, so that there is no way to identify a specific child. In our experience, it has been helpful to share the guidelines for how data will be collected and shared during a team meeting and then assign the tasks of collecting specific information to relevant members.

The consultant should not assume a position of authority when gathering data. The consultant's primary role is to help the team identify relevant data points and facilitate conversations about who will collect the data and how it will be shared and discussed. As the team members gather data, specify a place to store the information so it is accessible to all team members. We have typically used a shared Google Drive for this work, but other sharing platforms, such as Microsoft SharePoint, can work as well. We suggest that the consultant organize the shared files with clearly labeled titles and add a blank electronic copy of the TAGPEC to the sharing platform. In appendix B, we also provide a Behavior-Guidance Document Checklist (worksheet 4) that teams can use to organize their collected documentation.

The team will next use the TAGPEC to assess the quality of the policy, using all of the documents gathered as evidence. At this point, it is sometimes helpful for the consultant to clarify that the TAGPEC is not intended as a formal evaluation. It is a self-assessment tool that the team can use to identify where the policies are strong and where they can be improved to be more equitable and inclusive.

The consultant may recognize that the program needs additional data to assess its guidance policy and practices. If this is the case, the consultant can recommend gathering additional measures relevant to the goals of the program, such as measures of the following:

- Program climate

- Educator job satisfaction

- Office disciplinary referrals

- Rates of suspension and expulsion

- Absenteeism

- Academic scores

- Referrals to student success teams (SSTs)

- Referrals to special education

- Number of children receiving services from specialized services, such as mental health, speech, and occupational therapy

Some programs may also wish to gather information on family perspectives and/or satisfaction with behavior guidance using family surveys or focus groups. We urge the team to consider and understand the role of equity when selecting measures. The goal is to improve the program's overall discipline policy and practices, making them more equitable and developmentally appropriate—*not* to change students themselves. Inquire into whether the data you are collecting has been tested for bias and/or is appropriate for the population of students you are working with. Questions you might consider include the following:

- Does the data that you are collecting represent all students (gender, race, ethnicity, disability, language, religious background)?

- Are you using your data to shine a light on inequity or lack of inclusion?

- Are you identifying biases when using data?

With regard to identifying biases, it is natural for individuals to have biases—everyone does. What is key is being able to identify those biases and how they might be contributing to the ways the data is being interpreted. In one of my consultations with a program, for example, the program administrator had identified a particular student as "likely to continue to get into trouble." Having had the student in her office many times, she saw him as charming but constantly distracted due to his disability (ADHD). Her view of this student was that he was ultimately limited by his disability, but she didn't recognize that she held this bias toward him until another team member, the child's teacher, presented her perspective of the student as potentially gifted and bored.

A single piece of data—in this case, behavior-incident forms—can be interpreted multiple ways depending on the perspective of the individual reading them. Researchers call the tendency to be unaware of our own biases "bias blind spots." We can help to overcome these by ensuring that data conversations begin with each team member naming their bias(es) prior to sharing their perspective on the data. For example, in the previous example, the administrator might state, "I'm expecting to see that Student X will continue to be referred to my office for behavior incidents. I am working under the assumption that his ADHD is contributing to his behavior problems."

The process of selecting measures and collecting data can take time, so we suggest remaining flexible and open to exploring options and even changing measures if they aren't working for you. By taking a learning approach to the process, you allow your team to have the flexibility, time, and space to make informed decisions that will produce meaningful outcomes for your program.

✳ ✳ ✳

In summary, the third step of the TAGPEC five-step process is to work with the team to collect the program's existing documentation as it relates to behavior guidance and discipline. The consultant can assist in this process not by assuming the role of the expert but rather by asking questions about the program's existing documentation and ensuring that all team members have an opportunity to provide input. The consultant can also reassure the team that the purpose of this step is not to evaluate the program but to help them to identify their unique goals.

CHAPTER 8

Step 4: Assess the Quality of Your Behavior-Guidance Policy Using the TAGPEC

Once the team has collected the documents, they can begin the process of assessing the quality of the existing discipline policy using the TAGPEC. This step involves the following parts:

- Asking each team member to individually assess the guidance policy documents using the TAPGEC

- Meeting as a team to discuss individual findings and identifying collective strengths and considerations

- Creating an action plan based on the results

In our experience, it is helpful to have a meeting with the team to prepare them to use the TAGPEC. The consultant can begin by introducing the purpose of the TAGPEC, which is to assess the quality of the guidance policy. Since educators often have many demands placed on them, we are often open about the fact that the TAGPEC is not intended to be an evaluative tool, and that the final "score" isn't what matters. Instead, the purpose is to determine what in the policy is supporting students' social and emotional well-being, and what could be improved.

The consultant might then take some time to review the essential features and items of the TAGPEC with the team. If possible, we send out the tool to the team in advance so they can review it prior to the meeting. We like to review the entire tool and then provide some time for questions and answers. Some items may need clarification; in these instances, we suggest having examples of policy statements available to share. (See examples in our first book, *Effective Discipline Policies*.) We then establish a timeline for when the review will take place and when the meeting to discuss the findings will occur.

USE THE TAGPEC

We recommend having as many members of the team as possible assess the policy. The more input provided, the more likely the assessment will be accurate, as each team member may have a different perspective. The consultant should also complete the TAGPEC, but, again, they should not position themselves as the authority on the policy. Instead, the consultant completes the TAGPEC alongside the team using the documentation that the team has provided.

Because this is a self-assessment rather than a formal evaluation, it is not imperative that each person have the same response. As each team member completes the TAGPEC, they can enter their scores on the template found in appendix A. We do not emphasize the actual scores themselves but focus instead on individual items that need improvement.

SHARE FINDINGS

After each team member and the consultant has used the TAGPEC to assess the guidance policy, the team meets again to share and discuss their findings. The goal of this meeting is to describe and establish a baseline of the guidance policy. Each person must have space to articulate why they came to their response and an opportunity to discuss it with the group.

Often, teams are surprised to find that many of the behavioral principles and expectations that they hold are not explicit in their behavior-guidance policies. By focusing on the behavior policy in observable, measurable terms, the consultant can help the team identify any discrepancies between their current policy and their desired behavior-guidance model. The mission statement is also useful during this process as it can serve as a reminder of the desired goals.

The role of the consultant during the "findings" meeting is to help the team identify both the strengths and areas in need of improvement in the existing policy. There is no one process for sharing findings; rather, we suggest offering a couple of possibilities and allowing the group to decide. One possibility is to go through each TAGPEC item together, line by line, and ask members to share their scores and thoughts. This is a good time to discuss any differences and to hear multiple perspectives about each item. It is not essential that the team reaches a final decision about a score on an item; what is most important is that the team members can discuss the items. Another approach is to ask each team member what they identified as the strengths and the areas in need of improvement. Both approaches can help the team to identify items that may need further attention.

Once the team has shared their findings, the consultant helps facilitate a dialogue in which the team identifies specific problems—discrepancies between the revised mission and the actual policy documentation—to focus on. Team members may recognize when items on the TAGPEC are enacted in practice, but if the practices aren't explicit in the policy, there is no way to account for their being practiced consistently and with integrity.

When we worked with Dot to Dot, for example, the team recognized that each classroom had developed classroom agreements (expectations), but these were not shared across classrooms and were not necessarily consistent program-wide. As a result, the staff, students, and children did not have a common language for talking about behavior expectations. The team decided to discuss this with the staff and to work with them to create a set of common program-wide expectations that could then be written into the program's guidance policy.

SET GOALS AND CREATE AN ACTION PLAN

Programs may identify multiple areas where they want to improve their policy, and it's helpful to note them all. Noting the areas of concern, however, does not necessarily mean that all will be translated into specific goals. We learned about the importance of being realistic when working with the coaches from the Wisconsin Quality Rating Improvement Program. The role of these coaches was to consult with program administrators and teams on improving the quality and equity of their policies. They shared that during the process of working with teams, they realized that they needed to prioritize helping programs develop more primary and secondary prevention strategies and to focus on developing tertiary strategies at a later date. Another coach stated that one of her programs had decided to prioritize family engagement and focus on professional development the following year. The process of implementing a new behavior-guidance policy typically takes three to five years, so their strategy to prioritize allowed them to focus on certain goals while holding others for a later date.

We agree with taking a realistic approach to setting goals and implementation, even if it means that the guidance policy doesn't cover every item in the TAGPEC. The policy is intended to be a dynamic, living document that guides continued program improvement. The genuineness of the policy will help ensure that staff, educators, and families buy into the policy and stay committed to it throughout the process of implementing it.

It is natural when conducting a self-assessment for strong feelings to arise among team members regarding why challenging behaviors exist. During a consultation with an elementary school-based

PAUSE TO REFLECT

Let's say you, as the consultant, are with a behavior-guidance team as they are discussing their behavior-guidance goals. The administrator is very engaged and confident in the goals they are bringing forward. However, you notice that the classroom-teacher member is not engaged; his posture is somewhat slumped to the side of the chair, and he is doodling. What is coming up for you as the consultant in that moment? What are some hypotheses about the teacher's apparent disengagement?

preschool program, for example, teachers expressed frustration at the lack of support they felt from administration for children who had persistent challenging behaviors. They had shared their concerns about the lack of support with the school principal on multiple occasions but did not feel that solutions had been provided. They wondered why more training had not been offered, and why more teacher assistants and substitutes weren't hired so that they could have more time to help the children.

The principal, who was also part of the behavior-guidance team, felt defensive and shared her own challenges with severe staffing shortages. To move past blame and resistance, I validated both the teacher's and the principal's perspectives as important. It was helpful for both individuals to be able to hear about the other's unique challenges as it gave them a sense of empathy. The teacher understood that the principal cares about the teachers' needs but was having a difficult time finding qualified people to hire.

In my role as the consultant, I was able to reframe the issue as not residing in one individual, but rather as one that the team needed to consider as a whole. What could our work together contribute toward solving this problem? Could developing a stronger policy support the teacher in having a clear protocol for handling misbehavior? Could a stronger policy support the principal in getting additional resources from her district? The use of reframing helped the team move forward with the specific task ahead of them. Reframing is a strategy often used in consultation that can help team members adjust their perspective or experience of a situation. Reframing may include helping the team to focus on positives, adjust expectations, and share the experience from others' viewpoints. By reframing negative emotions and experiences, the consultant can help guide the conversation toward constructive goal setting and attainment. Questions to ask to help reframe a conversation can include the following:

- What positive things have come out of this situation?

- What effect have larger issues, such as the COVID-19 pandemic, had on your progress?

- What might the families be feeling about this?

By the end of the meeting, the team will have a short list of strengths and areas in need of improvement. The focus will be on what can be changed in the policy to reflect the ideals of the team, rather than on placing responsibility on individuals. The consultant can assist in this process by ending the meeting with a summary of these strengths and areas for improvement and by documenting them for the team in a shared drive or other format where it is accessible for everyone to view.

Develop an Action Plan

The final step of the self-assessment process is to develop an action plan. (See appendix B, Worksheet 5: Behavior-Guidance Policy Action Plan Template.) We have found that this step also requires a separate meeting. The purpose of the action plan is to think through short- and long-term goals for improving the guidance policy that are directly aligned with the data from the TAGPEC. The consultant can introduce the template and guide them through the process of completing it. If possible, the consultant should share the template on a large screen or shared drive while completing it with the team so that everyone can see each component. Alternatively, the consultant can distribute a blank copy of the action plan to each team member to complete as the team works.

For example, when working with Dot to Dot Preschool, we held a virtual meeting where I shared the action plan template over our shared Google Drive. We each had access to the drive and could refer to the findings of our TAGPEC as well as to our collective strengths and needs. Because the preschool program had not updated their policy in several years, their first action item was to revise the policy document. They determined that they wanted to create a separate behavior-guidance document that could be shared along with the parent and staff handbooks. Additionally, the team decided that two professional development trainings were needed: one that focused on the commitment statement and another that focused on training staff on the final policy. Finally, the team recognized that they did not have a plan for data collection and needed to introduce one or two simple data-collection tools to measure whether the policy was working.

When working with teams to develop an action plan, we often reference SMART goals as a way to ensure that we are staying focused on the outcomes (Doran, 1981). SMART goals are often used in business environments to help with goal setting. SMART is an acronym that stands for Specific, Measurable, Achievable, Realistic, and Timely. The action plan is based on these SMART goals with the addition of Resources:

- **Specific:** What will be accomplished? What actions will you take?

- **Measurable:** What data will we use to measure progress?

- **Achievable:** Is the goal doable? Do we have the necessary skills and resources?

- **Realistic and Resources:** How realistic is this goal? What resources are available and what are needed?

- **Time frame:** What is the time frame for accomplishing the goal?

WRITE THE GOALS

Specific: The consultant can help the team focus its attention and resources on writing goals that are most important to them so they can achieve their priorities. The consultant can also offer support by providing ideas for verbs that convey the direction that the program wants to go in. Many programs might say that they want to "improve" or "decrease" certain behaviors, for example, but these verbs don't clearly explain the specific action needed to make the change. Here is a list of sample verbs that might be useful:

Allocate	Communicate	Document	Formalize
Analyze	Complete	Educate	Generate
Apply	Create	Eliminate	Guide
Assemble	Cultivate	Encourage	Identify
Build	Delegate	Establish	Implement
Clarify	Deliver	Evaluate	Inspire
Collaborate	Demonstrate	Facilitate	Integrate
Collect	Design	Focus	Launch

Log	Plan	Report	Strengthen
Mentor	Prevent	Research	Summarize
Monitor	Propose	Respond	Support
Motivate	Publicize	Review	Target
Obtain	Recommend	Revise	Train
Organize	Recruit	Schedule	Translate
Participate	Reduce	Simplify	Unify
Pilot	Reorganize	Staff	

You can find more verbs related to SMART goals here: https://www.peoplegoal.com/glossary/smart-goals-verbs

Programs may wish to start the process with smaller goals and then work toward larger, long-term goals. With this in mind, we suggest guiding them toward documenting both short- and long-term goals so that they can keep both in mind as they move through the process.

Measurable: When writing the goals, the consultant can guide the team to develop goals that are measurable. By *measurable*, we are referring to the metrics that the team will use to determine whether each goal has been met. Having clear metrics makes each goal more "real" in the sense that it provides a concrete way to measure progress. Sometimes identifying a metric is challenging because there is no one clear data source or collection method for that goal. For instance, although the goal "train staff/educators/families" on the revised guidance policy is tangible, the team may need to determine how much training is needed, who will give the training, and how it will be delivered. Consultants can assist team members by offering a range of possibilities for the types of measures they can use to collect data for the goal. They may suggest, for example, quantitative measures, such as reductions in office referrals, suspensions, and expulsions, and qualitative measures, such as a revised guidance policy, parent testimonials, or educator surveys.

Achievable and Realistic with Available Resources: As the team works to develop goals and measures, the consultant can help them focus on whether the goal is achievable—within reach or realistic. Programs may believe in specific practices that align with the TAGPEC, for example, but the practices may not be achievable within the early stages of implementation. It is better to start with realistic goals and to add additional goals over time than to be overly ambitious and discouraged when a goal can't be achieved. The consultant can work with the team to identify the realities of their specific community setting. For example, if a program has limited administrative support or limited resources, then it does not help them to specify goals that require more than they can commit to. Along with being achievable, the goals need to be relevant to the specific program. If the program wants to include particular strategies for addressing challenging behavior, but the school district doesn't support those strategies, then that goal is likely not relevant. The consultant can work with the program team to create goals that are in alignment with the overall mission and vision for the program.

Timely: The consultant may need to provide guidance on the timeline for implementing each goal. One way that the consultant can help is to ask specific questions about each goal and what can be accomplished realistically within the allotted time frame. When discussing time frames, refer to the data-collection metrics that were identified to determine the proportion of time needed to achieve each goal. For example, if one goal is to reduce suspensions and expulsions by 50 percent, then the time frame could be within one academic year (10 months). Regarding the goal of creating a revised guidance policy, most programs that we have worked with have established a particular date (for example, May 30, 2022) to have it completed. Typically, this date falls before the start of new academic year, but theoretically it can be set at any point.

✳ ✳ ✳

In summary, the fourth step of the TAGPEC consultation model involves using the TAGPEC to assess the quality of the existing discipline policy and to develop an action plan. Other forms of data may also be introduced at this point if they are beneficial toward measuring the outcomes the program wants to achieve. As with other steps, the consultant completes the TAGPEC but does not serve as the "expert" on the findings. Rather, the consultant's role is to facilitate a conversation among staff about what they see as the strengths of the policy and what areas they believe need to be improved. This conversation sets the stage for the action plan, which is a detailed plan outlining who, how, and when the new behavior-guidance policy will be implemented.

CHAPTER 9

Step 5: Implement and Monitor the Program's Action Plan to Improve Its Behavior-Guidance Policy

In the fifth and final step, the team has three main tasks:

- Implement the specific action items (strategies) listed in the action plan.

- Introduce any professional or skill development needed to support the implementation of the goals.

- Monitor the implementation and plan revisions.

At this point, the program administrator must determine whether to continue to have the consultant facilitate the plan (typically this depends on funding) or to guide the program through this final stage themselves. In our experience, administrators have preferred to lead the implementation process with intermittent support from the consultant.

Implement the Action Items

Depending on the time frame for each goal, implementing the action items may occur in stages or all at once. In most programs we have worked with, implementation begins with creating a commitment statement, revising the guidance policy, and then offering professional development trainings to support implementing the policy at a programmatic level (all classrooms).

The program administrator is responsible for implementing the program's revised behavior-guidance policy and its corresponding practices. Using the action plan as a guide, the program administrator can follow through with the implementation with only occasional support from the consultant. Depending on the identified goals, this can take several weeks or, more often, months and is characterized by interactions between the program leader and the behavior-guidance team.

Implementing the discipline model also involves communicating the new or revised policy to all key members of the program, including educators and families. Communication is essential to ensure that all involved parties understand the policies and agree on their implementation before beginning the program. Programs can approach how they share the revised guidance policy in different ways. Some programs introduce the new policy at the start of the year, such as at a back-to-school orientation. Other programs, particularly those that are implementing the new policy mid-year, might hold a special meeting and/or provide a written message to families to share the new policy and provide opportunities for questions and input. They may, for example, do this via email or through meetings with the director.

Provide Professional or Skill Development

In the ECMHC model, the programmatic consultant provides two professional development workshops for staff that cater to the needs of the program. Often, the program leader wishes to use these workshops as opportunities to train the staff on the new policy. In other cases, the leader may wish to provide policy training and have the consultant supplement this with training on specialized topics related to social-emotional well-being, such as trauma-informed care and restorative justice. The specific topics can be arranged between the program leader and the consultant. In our experience, most programs benefit from some professional development training for staff so they can carry out the guidance model with integrity and consistency.

Monitor the Action Plan and Make Revisions as Needed

As the program administrator implements the plan, we recommend regular progress-monitoring meetings among the team to review new data and discuss progress toward each goal in relation to the timeline. If progress isn't being made as originally planned, the team can discuss possible reasons for this and can call on the consultant for additional feedback to ensure the timely completion of goals. Sometimes the team may determine that they need to revise the original goals and strategies. For example, if establishing a family liaison group was one of the original goals, but the team had problems recruiting family members, then the team may need to revise the goal to reflect family engagement in another way.

As the team is monitoring the data, we suggest the consultant prepare them by talking about the importance of implementation integrity. *Implementation integrity* refers to the degree to which the discipline model components are delivered as planned. The team can refer to the data to determine whether the program is making progress regarding the areas originally identified as concerns. Decisions related to integrity will involve continuing the strategies as planned, revising the strategies, and/or providing additional implementation support to staff or families to implement the plan as originally intended.

SUGGESTED ACTIVITIES FOR ONGOING BEHAVIOR-GUIDANCE POLICY MONITORING

Program-Level Consultation Activities:

- Meetings among behavior-guidance team to discuss policy, classroom practice, data, goals, plans, and collaboration activities such as mental-health services, disability services, and so on

- Meetings with staff to discuss policy and classroom practices

- Meetings with family to discuss policy and classroom practices

- Meetings with staff to discuss individual children

- Meetings with family to discuss individual children

- Formal trainings for staff related to policy and classroom practices

- Community outreach collaborations, trainings, and meetings

Data:

- Policy documents (original and revised)

- TAGPEC results

- Worksheet 1: Building a Behavior-Guidance Team

- Worksheet 2: Strengths, Needs, and Goals Interview Questions

- Worksheet 3: Behavior-Guidance Team Reflection Questions

- Worksheet 4: Behavior-Guidance Document Checklist

- Worksheet 5: Behavior-Guidance Policy Action Plan

- Worksheet 6: Record Keeping

- Number of office referrals for the month

- Number of in-school suspensions for the month

- Number of expulsions for the month

- Number of individual child screenings, assessments, or referrals

- Number of students receiving individualized behavior support

- Number of meetings with family members regarding behavior (including home visits)

- Testimonials (students/families/educators)

- Surveys (students/families/educators)

Once the team has completed each task, they can move into post-implementation planning to ensure that the changes made are sustained. Several options are available for how to design post-implementation plans. One strategy is to continue with the existing plan. However, in most cases, the team will need to modify it to some extent to reflect any progress made and/or new goals set. Another strategy is to reflect on the program's mission and values declaration and design a new set of goals that build, incrementally, on the progress made to date. A third strategy could be to determine what goals, if any, were not achieved in the original plan and to focus on those. As with the original plan, we suggest that the program leader co-construct action plans with the guidance team to ensure staff buy-in and support.

Regardless of which post-implementation strategy a program adopts, we highly recommended that the team decide on a process for record keeping. The consultant can provide the team with the record-keeping forms found in appendix B and can suggest other record-keeping forms as needed. Other forms that teams have found useful include templates for meeting agendas, meeting minutes, and email communications.

✳ ✳ ✳

In summary, the fifth and final step of the TAGPEC consultation model involves three primary tasks: implementing the items in the action plan, providing professional development to support implementation, and monitoring progress. In our experience, going through these three tasks is more cyclical than linear, and it may take up to five years before programs are in the maintenance or sustainability phase. We encourage programs to view this process as a long-term investment in children's well-being that, while it takes considerable time and resources, has a profound impact on their social-emotional and academic success.

A final note: We propose that the use of the TAGPEC programmatic consultation is an effective method for promoting the successful implementation of humanistic behavior-guidance approaches in early childhood education programs. The goal of programmatic consultation is to build the capacity of program leaders by supporting them in creating a positive program climate. The five-step process for engaging in programmatic consultation along with the TAGPEC tool can help facilitate meaningful conversations with program leaders and staff so that they are truly engaged in the process, and in the outcomes. Moving forward, we suggest that administrators who are implementing, or thinking about implementing, humanistic behavior-guidance approaches in their programs consider participating in our TAGPEC professional development trainings based on our proposed programmatic consultation model.

Appendix A:
The Teaching and Guidance Policy Essentials Checklist

Program's name: _____

Date filled out: _____

Completed by: _____

Role in program: _____

Instructions: This checklist is designed to identify different aspects of quality in early care and education guidance policies. This checklist can be completed by a trained program staff member or a specialist in early care and education.

For each question below, please check the response that best describes your program's guidance policy. Check *no* if the policy does not show evidence of addressing the item. Check *emerging* if your policy shows some evidence of addressing the item. Check *yes* if the policy shows clear evidence of addressing the item.

ESSENTIAL FEATURE 1: INTENTIONAL FOCUS ON TEACHING SOCIAL-EMOTIONAL SKILLS

Early childhood behavior-guidance policies should reflect an instructional, proactive approach to behavior guidance that supports the learning and practice of appropriate prosocial behavior of all children, regardless of individual differences and/or cultural and linguistic background.

Item 1: The policy clearly states that the goal of behavior guidance is to teach social-emotional skills to all children.

☐ Yes ☐ Emerging ☐ No

Item 2: The policy clearly describes the role of the teacher in proactively teaching all children social-emotional skills.

☐ Yes ☐ Emerging ☐ No

Item 3: The policy clearly describes the role of positive and consistent interactions among teachers and children in promoting positive behavior.

☐ Yes ☐ Emerging ☐ No

Item 4: Multiple, evidence-based, developmentally, culturally, and linguistically appropriate strategies are described.

☐ Yes ☐ Emerging ☐ No

ESSENTIAL FEATURE 2: INCLUSIVE, DEVELOPMENTALLY, CULTURALLY, AND LINGUISTICALLY APPROPRIATE LEARNING ENVIRONMENT

Early childhood behavior-guidance policies should describe the importance of an inclusive, developmentally, culturally, and linguistically appropriate learning environment that is predictable, engaging, and relationship based.

Item 5: The policy presumes placement of children with behavioral challenges in inclusive settings.

☐ Yes   ☐ Emerging   ☐ No

Item 6: The policy prohibits discrimination based on a child's characteristics, such as race, gender, and presence of disability.

☐ Yes   ☐ Emerging   ☐ No

Item 7: The policy clearly describes the importance of emotionally and instructionally responsive teacher-child relationships as essential to preventing challenging behaviors.

☐ Yes   ☐ Emerging   ☐ No

Item 8: The policy emphasizes the importance of sufficient and active adult supervision of all children.

☐ Yes   ☐ Emerging   ☐ No

Item 9: The policy describes the need for staff to continuously (at all times) monitor and respond to children's behavior.

☐ Yes   ☐ Emerging   ☐ No

Item 10: The policy clearly describes the use of ecological arrangements (classroom environment and materials) as a means for promoting positive, prosocial behavior.

☐ Yes   ☐ Emerging   ☐ No

Item 11: The policy clearly describes the need for a predictable, intentional, and developmentally appropriate daily schedule, such as small- and large-group times, carefully planned transitions, and child- and adult-initiated activities.

☐ Yes   ☐ Emerging   ☐ No

Item 12: The policy clearly describes the value of an engaging curriculum that takes a strengths-based view of culture and language as a deterrent to challenging behavior.

☐ Yes　　☐ Emerging　　☐ No

ESSENTIAL FEATURE 3: SETTING BEHAVIORAL EXPECTATIONS

Early childhood behavior-guidance policies should describe clear and consistent expectations for behavior that are culturally and linguistically appropriate.

Item 13: The policy has clearly stated program-wide behavioral expectations that are developmentally appropriate and reflect the natural learning abilities typically associated with the age groups of children served. If this item is answered *no*, then items 14–17 must be answered *no.*

☐ Yes　　☐ Emerging　　☐ No

Item 14: Behavioral expectations are stated positively and emphasize what children can and should do rather than what they cannot do.

☐ Yes　　☐ Emerging　　☐ No

Item 15: Behavioral expectations are designed to promote children's self-regulation, supporting external to internal foci from staff to self.

☐ Yes　　☐ Emerging　　☐ No

Item 16: The policy describes the need for clearly defined expectations that are observable and measurable at the classroom level.

☐ Yes　　☐ Emerging　　☐ No

Item 17: The policy describes the need for a connection between program-level behavioral expectations and classroom expectations.

☐ Yes　　☐ Emerging　　☐ No

Item 18: The policy clearly describes practices that are unacceptable for use by staff, such as humiliation; depriving meals, snacks, or rest; restraint; seclusion; and so on. Some states ban suspension and expulsion in early childhood programs. Please check your state's regulations.

☐ Yes　　☐ Emerging　　☐ No

ESSENTIAL FEATURE 4: PREVENTING AND ADDRESSING CHALLENGING BEHAVIORS USING A TIERED MODEL OF INTERVENTION

Early childhood behavior-guidance policies should identify culturally and linguistically appropriate primary, secondary, and tertiary preventative and intervention practices for promoting prosocial behavior and reducing challenging behavior in young children.

Item 19: Procedures are in place to screen children for behavioral concerns.

☐ Yes　　☐ Emerging　　☐ No

Item 20: The policy clearly describes the need to understand the reason(s) behind a child's challenging behavior, such as unmet needs for food, sleep, or safety or as a response to trauma.

☐ Yes　　☐ Emerging　　☐ No

Item 21: The policy clearly describes primary strategies to teach and reinforces prosocial behaviors in all children (see Items 1–12).

☐ Yes　　☐ Emerging　　☐ No

Item 22: The policy describes targeted secondary strategies, such as the use of social-skills curricula and intentional small-group instruction, for children who are at risk for problem behaviors.

☐ Yes　　☐ Emerging　　☐ No

Item 23: The policy clearly describes the use of tertiary strategies, such as developing a behavior-support plan, early childhood mental-health consultation, trauma-informed care, functional behavioral assessments that are research-based and culturally responsive, and referral for additional assessment, for helping children who exhibit chronic and intense problem behaviors.

☐ Yes　　☐ Emerging　　☐ No

Item 24: The policy describes the necessity of service coordination through intra- and interagency collaboration to mitigate behavioral challenges and to promote social-emotional competence.

☐ Yes　　☐ Emerging　　☐ No

Item 25: The policy assures privacy and confidentiality of personal information about behavioral assessment and intervention.

☐ Yes   ☐ Emerging   ☐ No

ESSENTIAL FEATURE 5: WORKING WITH FAMILIES

Early childhood behavior-guidance policies should reflect joint decision making, family priorities that foster family quality of life, and the needs of all family members.

Item 26: The policy promotes proactive rather than reactive collaborative, authentic relationships as a means of promoting social competence in children.

☐ Yes   ☐ Emerging   ☐ No

Item 27: The policy promotes staff-family collaboration in effectively dealing with challenging behavior, and families are given an opportunity to participate in developing and implementing interventions that are aligned with family priorities.

☐ Yes   ☐ Emerging   ☐ No

Item 28: The policy describes the need for obtaining contextually and culturally relevant information from families, such as at-home sleeping and eating habits, family events, and favorite toys and activities, to understand children's challenging behavior.

☐ Yes   ☐ Emerging   ☐ No

Item 29: The policy promotes embedding individual behavior-support-plan goals and objectives into family/home routines and activities.

☐ Yes   ☐ Emerging   ☐ No

ESSENTIAL FEATURE 6: STAFF TRAINING AND PROFESSIONAL DEVELOPMENT

Early childhood behavior-guidance policies should ensure that staff have access to training and technical assistance in implementing policy guidelines and promoting the social competence of young children.

Item 30: The policy describes practices that are in place to ensure that staff understand and can articulate the behavior-guidance policy.

☐ Yes   ☐ Emerging   ☐ No

Item 31: The policy describes a process for ongoing professional-development opportunities to support staff in the use of evidence-based prevention and intervention strategies.

☐ Yes ☐ Emerging ☐ No

Item 32: The policy describes the intent of the program to ensure that staff have a strong understanding of culture, diversity, equity, and inclusion and are provided opportunities to engage in self-reflection and ongoing professional development that encourage awareness of implicit and explicit biases that may affect their work with children and families.

☐ Yes ☐ Emerging ☐ No

ESSENTIAL FEATURE 7: USE OF DATA FOR CONTINUOUS IMPROVEMENT

Early childhood behavior-guidance policies should reference the use of a data-collection system by which the relative success or failure of the behavior-guidance policy will be evaluated.

Item 33: Policy-evaluation procedures are in place and clearly describe how the success or failure of the policy will be measured.

☐ Yes ☐ Emerging ☐ No

Item 34: The policy describes how data will be used to engage in continuous improvement to ensure that practices are in line with the intent of the behavior-guidance policy and to pin-point concerns, track progress, and ensure equity for all children.

☐ Yes ☐ Emerging ☐ No

Do you have any concerns about your program's guidance policy?

☐ No   ☐ Some   ☐ Yes

If you responded *some* or *yes*, please describe your concerns below.

_____

_____

_____

_____

_____

_____

Scoring the TAGPEC

STEPS

Step 1: Calculate score total. *No* = 0 *Emerging* = 1 *Yes* = 2

Step 2: Sum all of the item scores to get a total score.

Step 3: Enter the essential feature scores on the summary section.

Step 4: Enter the total score on the summary section.

Step 5: Higher item scores are strengths.

SUMMARY SECTION

Essential Feature	Subscale Total Score	Number of Items	Average Score
EF 1: Intentional Teaching Approach Item 1: _____ Item 2: _____ Item 3: _____ Item 4: _____		÷ 4	=
EF 2: Developmentally Appropriate Learning Environment Item 5: _____ Item 6: _____ Item 7: _____ Item 8: _____ Item 9: _____ Item 10: _____ Item 11: _____ Item 12: _____		÷ 8	=
EF 3: Setting Behavioral Expectations Item 13: _____ Item 14: _____ Item 15: _____ Item 16: _____ Item 17: _____ Item 18: _____		÷ 6	=
EF 4: Tiered Model of Intervention Item 19: _____ Item 20: _____ Item 21: _____ Item 22: _____ Item 23: _____ Item 24: _____ Item 25: _____		÷ 7	=
EF 5: Working with Families Item 26: _____ Item 27: _____ Item 28: _____ Item 29: _____		÷ 4	=

Essential Feature	Subscale Total Score	Number of Items	Average Score
EF 6: Staff Training and Professional Development Item 30: _____ Item 31: _____ Item 32: _____		$\div 3$	=
EF 7: Data Monitoring and Improvement Item 33: _____ Item 34: _____		$\div 2$	=

Total: _____		$\div 34$	=

COMMENTS SECTION

Policy Strengths:

_____

_____

_____

_____

_____

_____

_____

_____

_____

Policy Areas for Improvement:

_____

_____

_____

_____

_____

_____

_____

_____

_____

Developing and Implementing Effective Discipline Policies

Appendix B: TAGPEC Workbook

WORKSHEET 1: BUILDING A BEHAVIOR-GUIDANCE TEAM

Possible behavior-guidance team members:

- Administrator: Director, Principal, Assistant Director, Assistant Principal

- Office Staff

- Support Staff

- Classroom Teacher

- RTI Coordinator

- Special Education Teacher

- Parents or Guardians

- School Psychologist

- School Counselor or School Social Worker

- Invited Specialists, such as Behavior Coach, Consultants, Foster Youth Services Staff, and Social Worker

Following is a table of team-member roles and responsibilities, to be completed by the coordinator or leader during the first behavior-guidance meeting.

Team Role	Team Responsibilities	Team Members' Names
Coordinator/ Leader	• Schedule meetings, communicate meeting dates and agendas to members • Lead meetings: - call meetings to order - introduce team members - review purpose of meeting - summarize problem areas - lead group in problem solving - monitor time - monitor progress	_____
Recorder	• Record problem-solving process • Note contributions made by all team members	_____
Assessor	• Rate school or program's guidance policy using TAGPEC	_____
Data Manager	• Collect data related to behavioral issues, such as behavior incident reports, referrals, behavior-support plans, suspensions and expulsions, and TAGPEC data • Enter new data in file • Maintain data in file	_____
Program or School Team Member	• Share perspective on behavior guidance from the program or school perspective • Collaborate with team to problem solve solution	_____
Parent Team Member	• Share perspective on behavior guidance from the parent perspective • Collaborate with team to problem solve solutions	_____
Invited Specialists	• Share perspective on behavior guidance from the specialists' perspectives • Collaborate with team to problem solve solutions • Recommend specialists for tier 3 interventions	_____

WORKSHEET 2: STRENGTHS, NEEDS, AND GOALS INTERVIEW QUESTIONS

- What do you see as the current strengths of your program?

- What interests, concerns, and/or problems are you hoping to address as part of the programmatic consultation?

- What do you ultimately want to see as a result of the programmatic consultation?

- What do you see as some of the barriers to your reaching the results you want?

- What strategies have you already tried?

- What resources does your program need to help you achieve those results?

- What would make it likely or possible for staff and other stakeholders to participate in programmatic activities such as trainings?

- What barriers to participation do you foresee?

- What information do you need to make decisions about the program?

- Anything else that you want to share about the programmatic consultation?

WORKSHEET 3: BEHAVIOR-GUIDANCE TEAM REFLECTION QUESTIONS*

This worksheet presents sample questions for reflective thinking during a behavior-guidance policy meeting. The intent is to help staff:

- explore their own discipline experiences,

- develop an understanding of the various perspectives of discipline held by culturally diverse parents and family members,

- identify how culture affects their perspectives on discipline, and

- consider how their views of discipline affect their interactions with children in their work.

These questions should be considered only as a starting point for discussion and further study; they do not represent a comprehensive approach to the issues.

Behavior-Guidance Team Meeting Reflection Questions

1   What do you remember about how your parents or guardians disciplined you growing up? How might your personal background or culture influence your thinking about discipline and child guidance?

2   When do your values and beliefs about discipline conflict with those of families enrolled in your program? How can you discuss these differences in values and beliefs with families in order to benefit the children?

3   What social and emotional skills and behaviors do parents in your program value in their children?

4   What systems or strategies does your program currently have in place to obtain additional information about how discipline is practiced at home and how behavioral interventions are practiced at home?

5   In what ways do the policies and practices of your program reflect information about the families in your program?

6   Reflect on your program's policy statement regarding discipline/guidance. Is there other information that you feel is important that has not yet been included in the definition? Explain.

7   How are families invited by your program to participate in their children's social, emotional, and academic success? Is this reflected in your policy?

8   Does your program have a self-evaluation process for reviewing the effectiveness of your discipline/guidance policy? Please describe.

9   What opportunities do various members of the program and community have to provide input on the guidance policy?

10 What opportunities do program staff have to participate in trainings related to behavior-guidance practices that are embedded in the program's or school's guidance policy?

*Adapted from *Multicultural Principles for Head Start Programs Serving Children Ages Birth to Five*, Department of Health and Human Services, Office of Head Start.

WORKSHEET 4: BEHAVIOR-GUIDANCE DOCUMENT CHECKLIST

Once you have collected all of the available documents on behavior guidance within your program, it is time for you and your team to evaluate each item in relation to your newly developed commitment statement. To do this, we suggest laying the physical documents on a large table and then going through them, one by one, asking the question, "How does this document support our belief and commitment to positive behavior guidance?" (Refer to your completed worksheet 3 to remind your team of your commitment statement.)

Use the document checklist to list the type of each document in the first column. In the second column, check whether or not the document fulfills an important element of your commitment statement. If it doesn't, then you will want to keep it for reference when you write your final policy draft. Use the third column to make notes about what is working and what is still needed for each of the documents.

One of the most important parts of this process is to determine whether your program is sending a consistent message that reflects your commitment statement. Does the information provided to staff in the staff manual reflect what is in the parent handbook? Is this information consistent with your referral process?

Behavior-Guidance Document Checklist

Type/Name of Document	Does document align with commitment statement? Yes No	Comments What is working? What needs improvement?

WORKSHEET 5: BEHAVIOR-GUIDANCE POLICY ACTION PLAN TEMPLATE

Create a "script" for your improvement effort and support implementation. Develop a work plan for each goal identified through the needs-assessment process. (Feel free to modify the form as needed to fit your unique context.) Distribute copies of the action plan to the members of the collaboration. Keep copies handy to bring to meeting to review and update regularly. You may decide to develop new plans for new phases of your improvement effort.

1   State your goal, and list your action steps.

2   Next, name who will be in charge of each action step.

3   Decide the timeline of each action step; when will each be completed?

4   List the resources you have available, then list the resources you still need. These may be human, financial, political, and so on.

5   List any potential barriers to your action steps. What individuals or organizations might resist?

6   List who will be involved in each action step and how and how often those team members will communicate.

7   Decide how you will show evidence of success—what are your benchmarks?

8   Decide on your evaluation process. List the measures by which you will determine that your goal has been reached.

Goal

_____

_____

_____

Action Steps

Step 1:

_____

Step 2:

_____

Step 3:

_____

Step 4:

_____

Step 5:

_____

Responsibilities

Step 1: _____

Step 2: _____

Step 3: _____

Step 4: _____

Step 5: _____

Timeline

Step 1: _____

Step 2: _____

Step 3: _____

Step 4: _____

Step 5: _____

Resources Available

Step 1: _____

Step 2: _____

Step 3: _____

Step 4: _____

Step 5: _____

Resources Needed

Step 1: _____

Step 2: _____

Step 3: _____

Step 4: _____

Step 5: _____

Potential Barriers

Step 1:

_____

Step 2:

_____

Step 3:

_____

Step 4:

_____

Step 5:

_____

Communication

Step 1:

_____

Step 2:

_____

Step 3:

_____

Step 4:

_____

Step 5:

_____

Evidence of Success

_____

_____

_____

_____

_____

Evaluation Process

_____

_____

_____

_____

_____

_____

WORKSHEET 6: RECORD KEEPING

Behavior-Guidance Meeting

Date: _____

Time: _____

Site: _____

Meeting called by: _____

Meeting format (circle one):   Virtual / In person

Facilitator: _____

Notetaker: _____

Attendees: _____

_____

Please read: _____

Please bring: _____

Appendix C: TAGPEC Five-Step Process Sample Timeline

WEEK ONE: DECEMBER 2-6

Program
- ☐ Meet with program director
- ☐ **Administer:** Strengths, Needs, and Goals Interview
- ☐ **Administer:** Building a Behavior-Guidance Team
- ☐ **Administer:** Behavior-Guidance Document Checklist; ask administrator to collect documents
- ☐ **Deliverable:** Book, *Effective Discipline Policies* by Longstreth and Garrity

Classroom

Meet with teacher and begin observations

WEEK TWO: DECEMBER 9-13

Program
- ☐ Meet with program director and behavior-guidance team
- ☐ **Administer:** Team Behavior-Guidance Reflection Questions
- ☐ **Administer:** Behavior-Guidance Document Checklist; complete as a team
- ☐ Briefly review what TAGPEC is and next steps (consultant will assess documents using the TAGPEC after the meeting and report results at the following meeting)

Classroom

Conduct classroom social-emotional and Pyramid-adherence observations

WEEK THREE: DECEMBER 16-20

Program
- ☐ Meet with program director and behavior-guidance team
- ☐ **Deliverable:** Review results of the TAGPEC with the team
- ☐ Program director and behavior-guidance team develop a Behavior-Guidance Commitment Statement using data from Week 1 assessments and TAGPEC
- ☐ Create an action plan based on TAGPEC results
- ☐ Briefly review next steps: consultant will draft a revised guidance policy and will share draft for editing with the program director and behavior-guidance team

Classroom
- ☐ Meet with teacher and identify 2 children
- ☐ Collect preconsultation teacher reports on children

WEEK FOUR: DECEMBER 30-JANUARY 3

Program	☐ **Deliverable:** Finalize revised guidance policy
Classroom	Conduct observational assessments of teacher-child interactions

WEEK FIVE: JANUARY 6-10

Program	☐ Support implementation of revised guidance policy; provide program director with support as needed
Classroom	Meet with parents and teachers

WEEK SIX: JANUARY 13-17

Program	☐ Support implementation of revised guidance policy; provide program director with support as needed
Classroom	☐ Meet with teacher about classroom and child action plans ☐ Meet with parents

WEEK SEVEN: JANUARY 20-24

Program	☐ **Deliverable:** Program-wide training: A Humanistic Approach to Behavior Guidance and the TAGPEC ☐ **Deliverable:** Revised guidance policy ☐ **Deliverable:** Program-wide training: The Impact of Trauma on Early Childhood Development and Learning and Addressing Children's Mental Health Concerns and Referrals
Classroom	☐ Support implementation of plan (modeling, coaching, revising) ☐ Follow up on referrals for children and families

WEEK EIGHT: JANUARY 27-31

Program
☐ Support implementation of revised guidance policy; provide program director with support as needed

Classroom
☐ Support implementation of plan (modeling, coaching, revising)
☐ Follow up on referrals for children and families

WEEK NINE: FEBRUARY 3-7

Program
☐ Support implementation of revised guidance policy; provide program director with support as needed

Classroom
☐ Support implementation of plan (modeling, coaching, revising)
☐ Follow up on referrals for children and families

WEEK TEN: FEBRUARY 10-14

Program
☐ Support implementation of revised guidance policy; provide program director with support as needed

Classroom
☐ Support implementation of plan (modeling, coaching, revising)
☐ Follow up on referrals for children and families

WEEK ELEVEN: FEBRUARY 17-21

Program
☐ Support implementation of revised guidance policy; provide program director with support as needed

Classroom
☐ **Deliverable:** Share observations of classroom/child
☐ **Deliverable:** Share teacher reports

WEEK TWELVE: FEBRUARY 24–28

Program
- ☐ Meet with program director and behavior-guidance team
- ☐ **Deliverable:** Review implementation of the TAGPEC with the team
- ☐ Revise an action plan based on the results of the TAGPEC

Classroom
- ☐ Meet with teacher providing follow-up observation feedback
- ☐ Report to administrator on pre and post assessments and ongoing support plan
- ☐ **Deliverable:** Ongoing support plan for next two weeks
- ☐ Meet with parents as needed

Appendix D: Resources

Culturally Responsive Practice

Derman-Sparks, Louise, Debbie LeeKeenan, and John Nimmo. 2015. *Leading Anti-Bias Early Childhood Programs: A Guide for Change.* New York: Teachers College Press.

Isik-Ercan, Zeynep. 2017. "Culturally Appropriate Guidance with Young Children." *Young Children* 72(1). https://www.naeyc.org/resources/pubs/yc/mar2017/culturally-appropriate-positive-guidance

Price, Charis L., and Elizabeth A. Steed. 2016. "Culturally Responsive Strategies to Support Young Children with Challenging Behavior." *Young Children* 71(5). https://www.naeyc.org/resources/pubs/yc/nov2016/culturally-responsive-strategies

Reflective Practice

Di Gennaro, Diana C., Erika M. Pace, Iolanda Zollo, and Paola Aiello. 2014. "Teacher Capacity Building through Critical Reflective Practice for the Promotion of Inclusive Education." *Problems of Education in the 21st Century* 60(1): 54–66.

Early Head Start National Resource Center. n.d. *A Collection of Tips on Becoming a Reflective Supervisor.* Washington, DC: Author. https://eclkc.ohs.acf.hhs.gov/sites/default/files/pdf/rs-supervisor-info-sheet.pdf

Hall, Pete, and Alisa Simeral. 2017. *Creating a Culture of Reflective Practice: Capacity-Building for Schoolwide Success.* Alexandria, VA: ASCD.

Heffron, Mary Claire, and Trudi Murch. 2011. *Reflective Supervision and Leadership in Infant and Early Childhood Programs.* Washington, DC: Zero to Three.

Heffron, Mary Claire, and Trudi Murch. 2013. *Finding the Words, Finding the Ways: Exploring Reflective Supervision and Facilitation.* San Francisco, CA: WestEd.

Kovacs, Louise, and Sarah Corrie. 2022. "Building Reflective Capability to Enhance Coaching Practice." In *Coaching Practiced.* Hoboken, NJ: John Wiley and Sons Ltd.

Rich, Robert A., and Sherion H. Jackson. 2006. "Building the Reflective Capacity of Practicing Principals." *AASA Journal of Scholarship and Practice* 2(4): 12–18.

Watts, Caroline L., et al. 2008. *Supportive Supervision: Promoting Staff and Family Growth through Positive Relationships.* Boston, MA: Children's Hospital Boston. https://eclkc.ohs.acf.hhs.gov/sites/default/files/pdf/supportive-supervision-promoting-staff-positive-relationships.pdf

Social-Emotional Well-Being and School Discipline

Education Northwest. 2018. "What the Research Says on Supporting the Social and Emotional Well-Being of Students." Education Northwest. https://educationnorthwest.org/resources/what-research-says-supporting-social-and-emotional-well-being-students

Gregory, Anne, and Edward Fergus. 2017. "Social and Emotional Learning and Equity in School Discipline." *The Future of Children* 27(1): 117–136.

Skiba, Russell J., and Daniel J. Losen. 2016. "From Reaction to Prevention: Turning the Page on School Discipline." *American Educator* 39(4): 4–11.

Trauma-Informed Training for Coaches and Consultants

Neurosequential Model in Education. https://www.neurosequential.com/nme

Neurosequential Model in Reflection and Supervision. https://www.neurosequential.com/nmrs

Trauma-Informed Resources for Schools

The National Child Traumatic Stress Network. 2008. *Child Trauma Toolkit for Educators*. Los Angeles, CA & Durham, NC: National Center for Child Traumatic Stress. https://www.nctsn.org/sites/default/files/resources//child_trauma_toolkit_educators.pdf

The National Child Traumatic Stress Network. 2008. *Psychological and Behavioral Impact of Trauma for Preschoolers*. Los Angeles, CA & Durham, NC: National Center for Child Traumatic Stress. English: https://www.nctsn.org/resources/psychological-and-behavioral-impact-trauma-preschool-children Spanish: https://www.nctsn.org/resources/impacto-psicologico-y-conductual-del-trauma-ninos-preescolares

The National Child Traumatic Stress Network. 2020. *Supporting Schools to Test and Implement Tailored Trauma-Informed Practices*. Video. Los Angeles, CA & Durham, NC: National Center for Child Traumatic Stress. https://www.nctsn.org/resources/supporting-schools-to-test-and-implement-tailored-trauma-informed-practices

Trauma-Informed Resources for Teachers and Classrooms

Eber, Lucille, et al. 2020. *Integrating a Trauma-Informed Approach within a PBIS Framework*. Eugene, OR: Center on PBIS, University of Oregon. https://www.pbis.org/resource/integrating-a-trauma-informed-approach-within-a-pbis-framework

Perry, Bruce D., Erin Hambrick, and Robert D. Perry. 2016. "The NMC Ten Tip Series: The Intimacy Barrier." Neurosequential Network. https://www.bdperry.com/_files/ugd/5cebf2_93fea3b2390b416aa73570db72e67a73.pdf

Restorative Justice

Adair, Jennifer K., and Shubhi Sachdeva. 2021. "Agency and Power in Young Children's Lives: Five Ways to Advocate for Social Justice as an Early Childhood Educator." *Young Children* 76(2): 40–48.

Breedlove, Meghan, Jihyeon Choi, and Brett Zyromski. 2021. "Mitigating the Effects of Adverse Childhood Experiences: How Restorative Practices in Schools Support Positive Childhood Experiences and Protective Factors." *The New Educator* 17(3): 223–241.

Elias, Maurice J. 2016. "Why Restorative Practices Benefit All Students." Edutopia. https://www.edutopia.org/blog/why-restorative-practices-benefit-all-students-maurice-elias

Essien, Idara, and J. Luke Wood. 2022. "Suspected, Surveilled, Singled-Out, and Sentenced: An Assumption of Criminality for Black Males in Early Learning." *Journal of Negro Education* 91(1): 65–82.

Lawrence, Erica, and Tracy Hinds. 2016. "From Punish and Discipline to Repair and Restore." *Principal* Nov.–Dec.: 23–34. https://www.naesp.org/sites/default/files/LawrenceHinds_ND16.pdf

Lyubanski, Mikhail. 2016. "New Study Reveals Six Benefits of School Restorative Justice." *Psychology Today*. https://www.psychologytoday.com/us/blog/between-the-lines/201605/new-study-reveals-six-benefits-school-restorative-justice

Velez, Gabriel, and Theo Gavrielides, eds. 2022. *Restorative Justice: Promoting Peace and Wellbeing*. Peace Psychology Book Series. Cham, Switzerland: Springer Nature.

References and Recommended Reading

Cohen, Elena, and Roxane K. Kaufmann. 2005. *Early Childhood Mental Health Consultation*. DHHS Pub. No. CMHS-SVP0151. Rockville, MD: Center for Mental Health Services, Substance Abuse and Mental Health Services Administration.

Doran, George T. 1981. "There's a S.M.A.R.T. Way to Write Management Goals and Objectives." *Management Review* 70: 35–36.

Drawing Change. 2019. "Co-Creating Community Agreements in Meetings." Drawing Change. https://drawingchange.com/co-creating-community-agremeents-in-meetings/

Garrity, Sarah, and Sascha Longstreth. 2020. "Using the Teaching and Guidance Policy Essentials Checklist to Develop Culturally and Linguistically Appropriate Behavior-Guidance Policies." *Early Childhood Education Journal* 48(1): 71–77.

Garrity, Sarah, Sascha Longstreth, and Lisa Linder. 2016. "An Examination of the Quality of Behavior-Guidance Policies in NAEYC-Accredited Early Care and Education Programs." *Topics in Early Childhood Education* 37(2): 94–106.

Garrity, Sarah, Sascha Longstreth, Nina Salcedo-Potter, and April Staub. 2015. "Using the Teaching and Guidance Policy Essentials Checklist to Build and Support Effective Early Childhood Systems." *Early Childhood Education Journal* 44(3): 209–216.

Hunter, Amy, Anna Davis, Deborah Perry, and Wendy Jones. 2016. *The Georgetown Model of Early Childhood Mental Health Consultation for School-Based Settings*. Washington, DC: Center for Child and Human Development, Georgetown University. https://www.ecmhc.org/documents/FCC_SB%20ECMHC%20Manual.pdf

Kendi, Ibram X. 2019. *How to Be an Antiracist*. New York: One World.

Iruka, Iheoma U., Stephanie M. Curenton, Tonia R. Durden, and Kerry-Ann Escayg. 2020. *Don't Look Away: Embracing Anti-Bias Classrooms*. Lewisville, NC: Gryphon House.

Longstreth, Sascha, and Sarah Garrity. 2018. *Effective Discipline Policies: How to Create a System that Supports Young Children's Social-Emotional Competence*. Lewisville, NC: Gryphon House.

Love, Bettina. 2019. *We Want to Do More Than Survive: Abolitionist Teaching and the Pursuit of Educational Freedom*. Boston, MA: Beacon Press.

Maslow, Abraham. 1943. "A Theory of Human Motivation." *Psychological Review* 50(4): 370–396.

NAEYC. 2019. *Advancing Equity in Early Childhood Education*. Position statement. https://www.naeyc.org/sites/default/files/globally-shared/downloads/PDFs/resources/position-statements/advancingequitypositionstatement.pdf

NAEYC. 2020. *Developmentally Appropriate Practice*. Position statement. Washington, DC: NAEYC.

NAEYC. 2022. *Developmentally Appropriate Practice in Early Childhood Programs Serving Children from Birth through Age 8*. 4th edition. Washington, DC: NAEYC.

NAEYC, et al. 2016. *Standing Together against Suspension and Expulsion in Early Childhood: A Joint Statement.* https://www.naeyc.org/sites/default/files/globally-shared/downloads/PDFs/resources/topics/Standing%20Together.Joint%20Statement.FINAL__9_0.pdf

Pub. L. 113-186. *Child Care and Development Block Grant of 2014.*

Rogers, Carl. 1961. *On Becoming a Person: A Therapist's View of Psychotherapy.* London, UK: Constable.

Shahmoon-Shanok, Rebecca. 1991. "The Supervisory Relationship: Integrator, Resource, and Guide." *Zero to Three* 12: 16–19.

Shahmoon-Shanok, Rebecca. 2006. "Reflective Supervision for an Integrated Model: What, Why, and How?" In *Mental Health in Early Intervention.* Baltimore, MD: Paul H. Brookes Publishing.

Substance Abuse and Mental Health Services Administration. 2014. *Expert Convening on Infant and Early Childhood Mental Health Consultation.* Rockville, MD: SAMHSA Headquarters.

Turnbull, Ann, Rud Turnbull, Michael L. Wehmeyer, and Karrie A. Shogren. 2020. *Exceptional Lives: Practice, Progress, and Dignity in Today's Schools.* 9th edition. Hoboken, NJ: Pearson.

US Department of Education, Office for Civil Rights. 2014. *Civil Rights Data Collection: Data Snapshot: Early Childhood Education.* Issue Brief No. 2. Washington, DC: U.S. Department of Education.

US Department of Health and Human Services, Administration for Children and Families. 2015. Head Start Early Learning Outcomes Framework: Ages Birth to Five. Washington, DC: Office of Head Start, Administration for Children and Families. https://eclkc.ohs.acf.hhs.gov/sites/default/files/pdf/elof-ohs-framework.pdf

US Department of Health and Human Services, Office of Head Start, Administration for Children and Families. 2016. *Head Start Program Performance Standards.* Washington, DC: Office of Head Start, Administration for Children and Families.

US Department of Health and Human Services and US Department of Education. 2014. *Policy Statement on Expulsion and Suspension Policies in Early Childhood Settings.* Washington, DC: US Department of Health and Human Services. https://www2.ed.gov/policy/gen/guid/school-discipline/policy-statement-ece-expulsions-suspensions.pdf

Index